Dark Room: San Francisco Sex and Protest, 1988–2003

Phyllis Christopher

Book Works

To all of the models and performers I have collaborated with over the years.
You said no to your fears and yes to your bliss and San Francisco opened her loving arms.

LEPHONE
TE

GAY
+
FIGHTING
BAC
TOP
ANTI-GAY
VIOLENCE

GOD
IS A
BLACK
LESBIAN

OUR
RIGHT
TO
GRIEVE
OUR
RIGHT
TO
LOVE
OUR
RIGHT
TO
GRIEVE
OUR
RIGHT
TO
LOVE

POLICE

QUEE

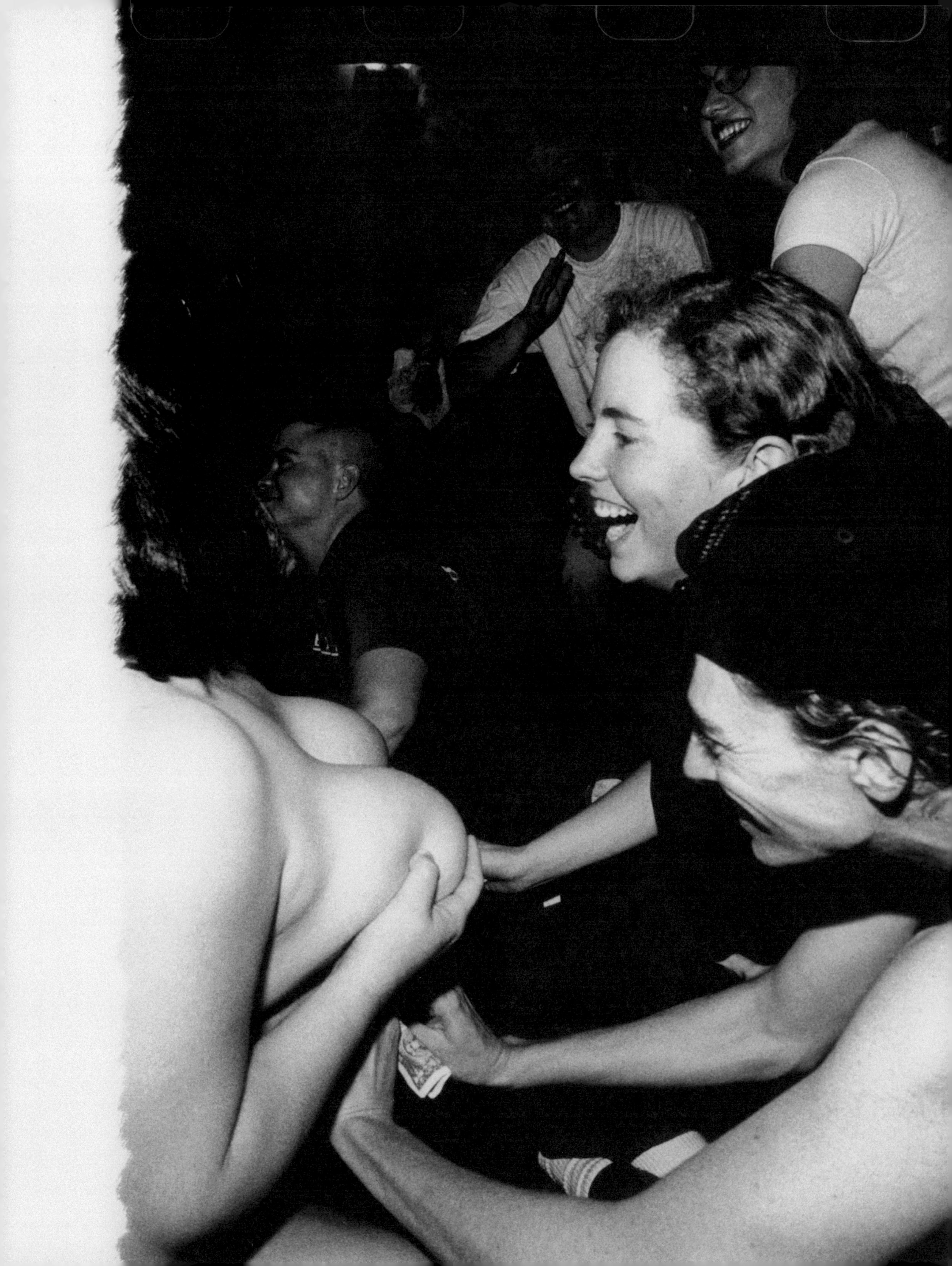

ASSIMILATE
MY FIST
EAT PUSSY

ROBERT MAPPLETHORPE
IS THE
MESSIAH.

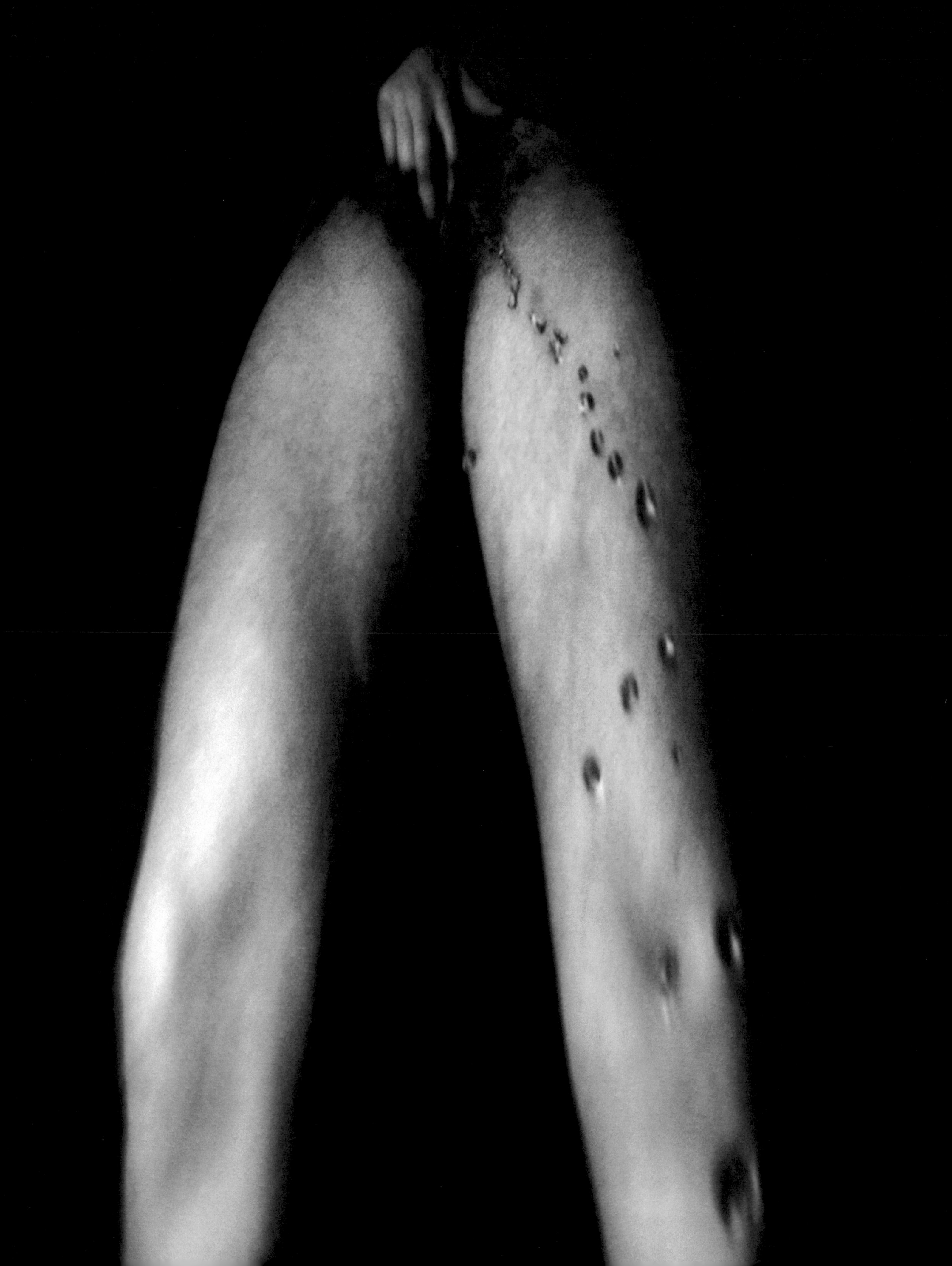

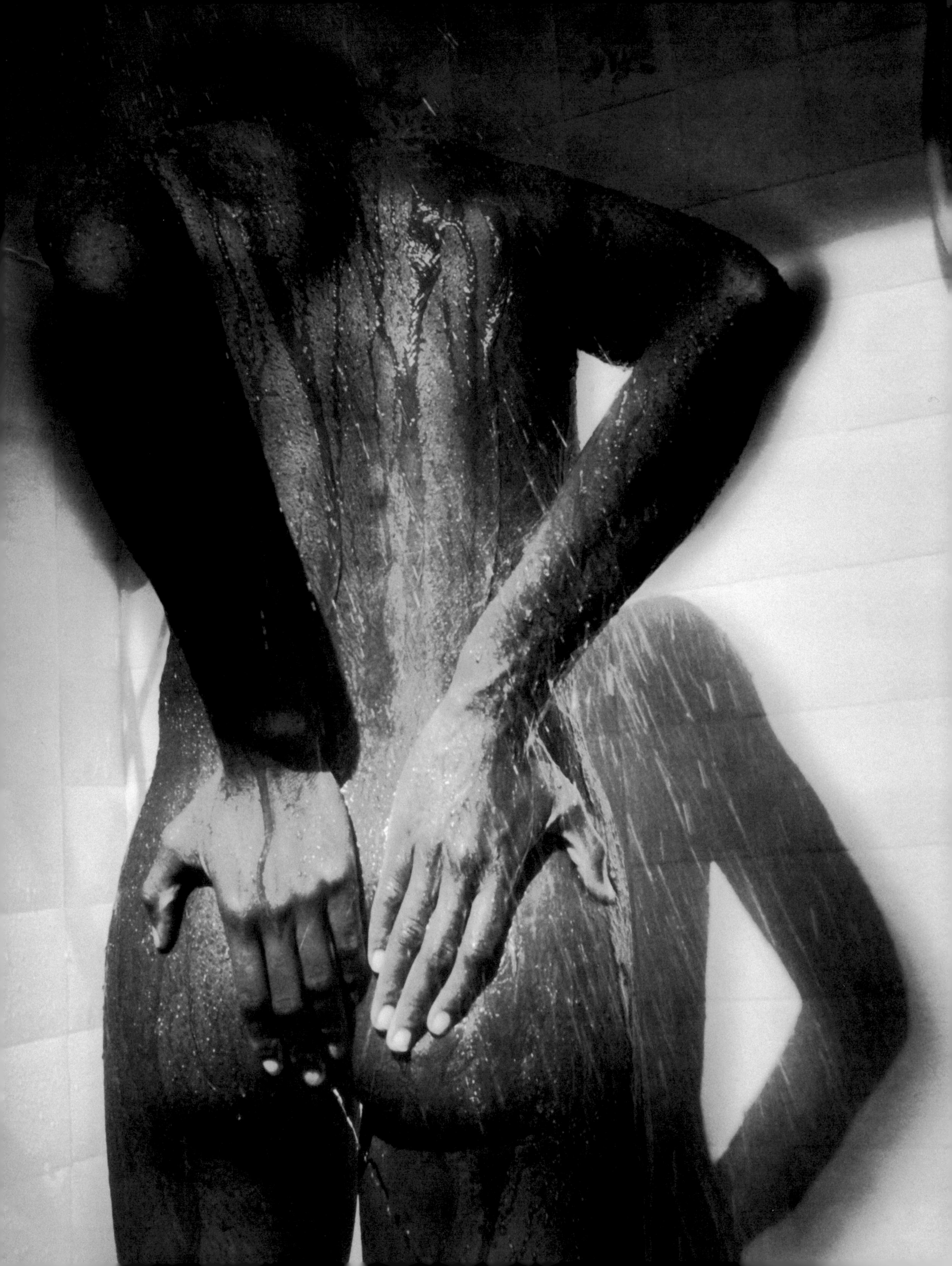

NO
PAR
ANY

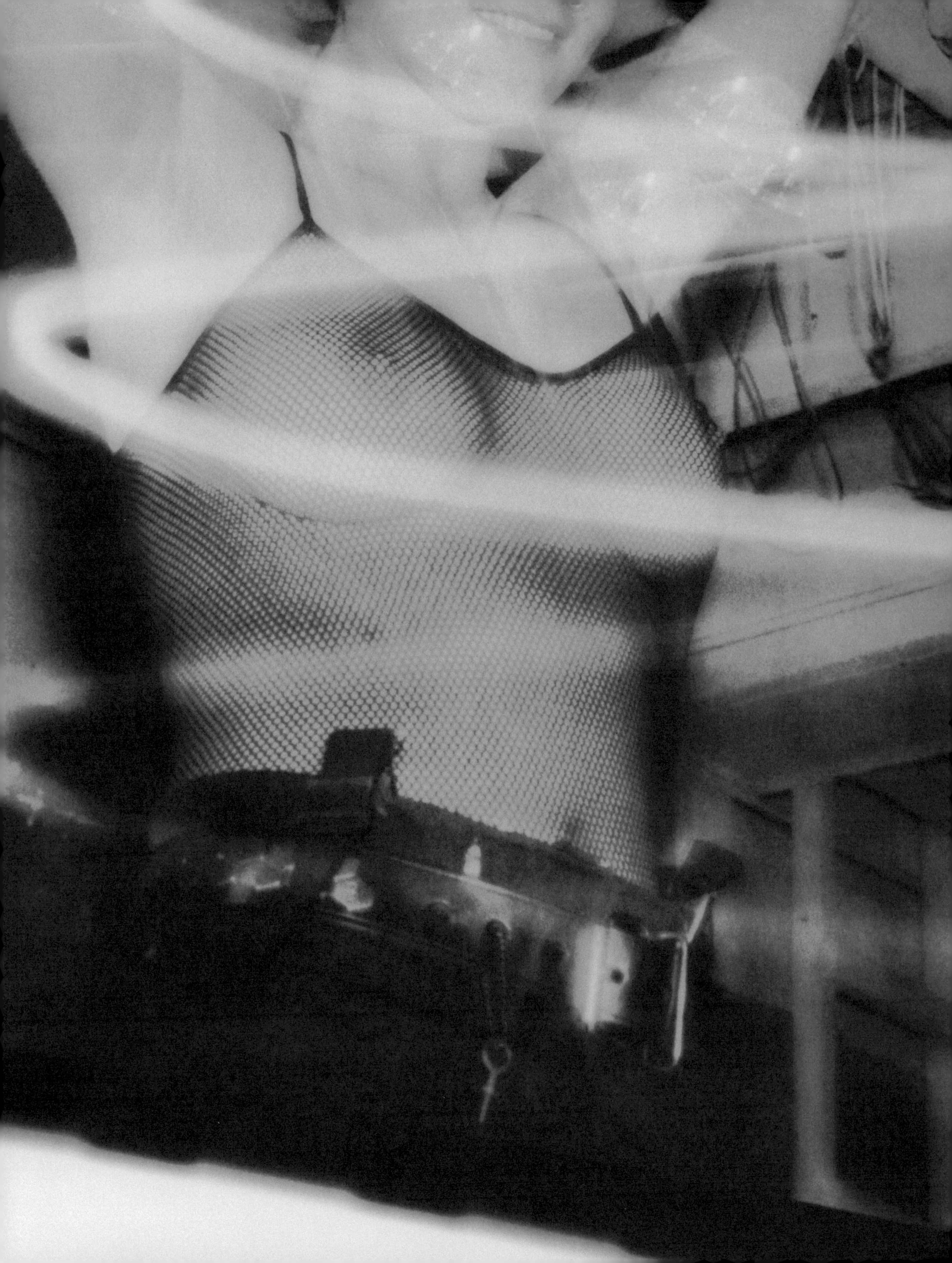

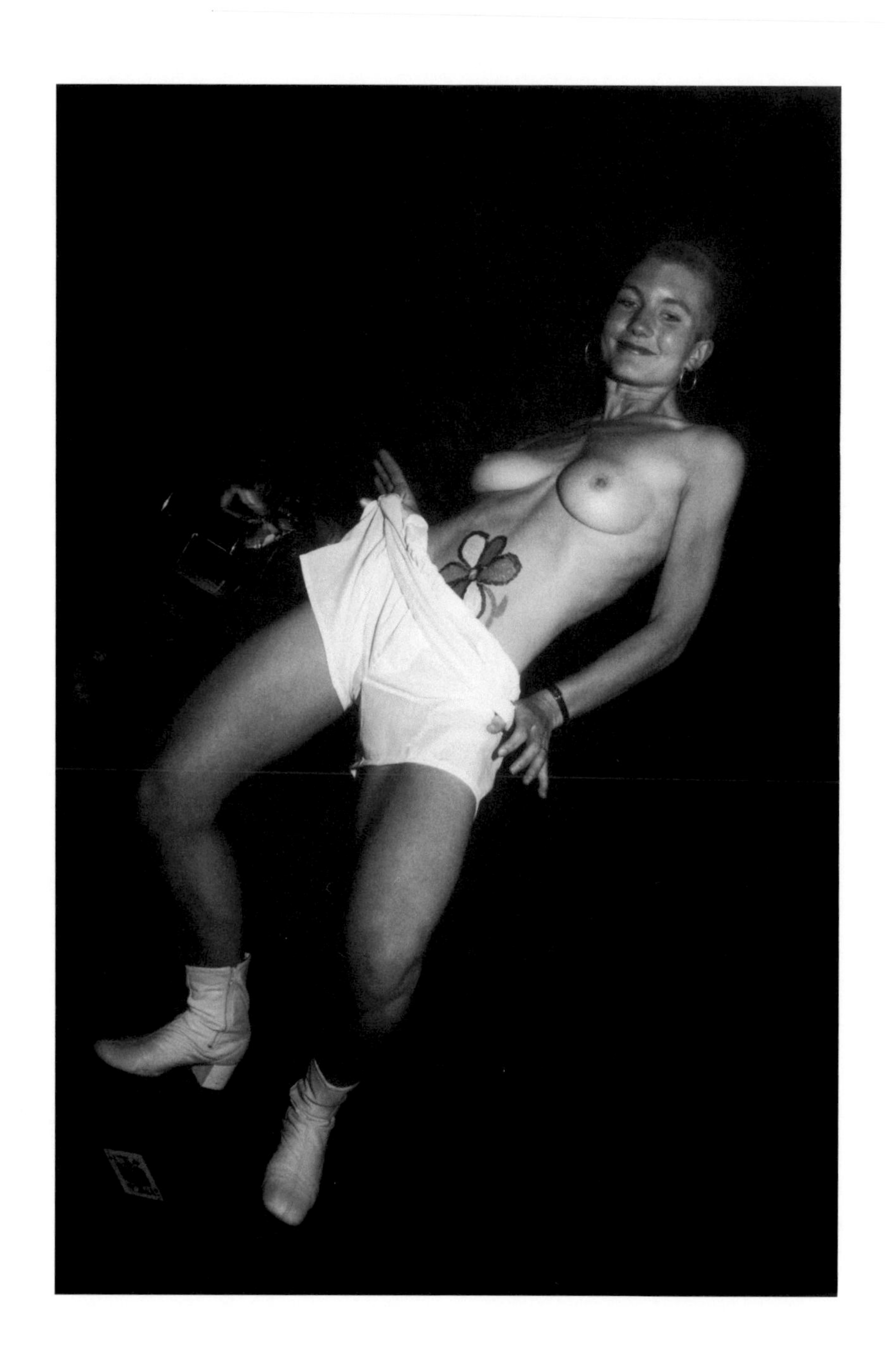

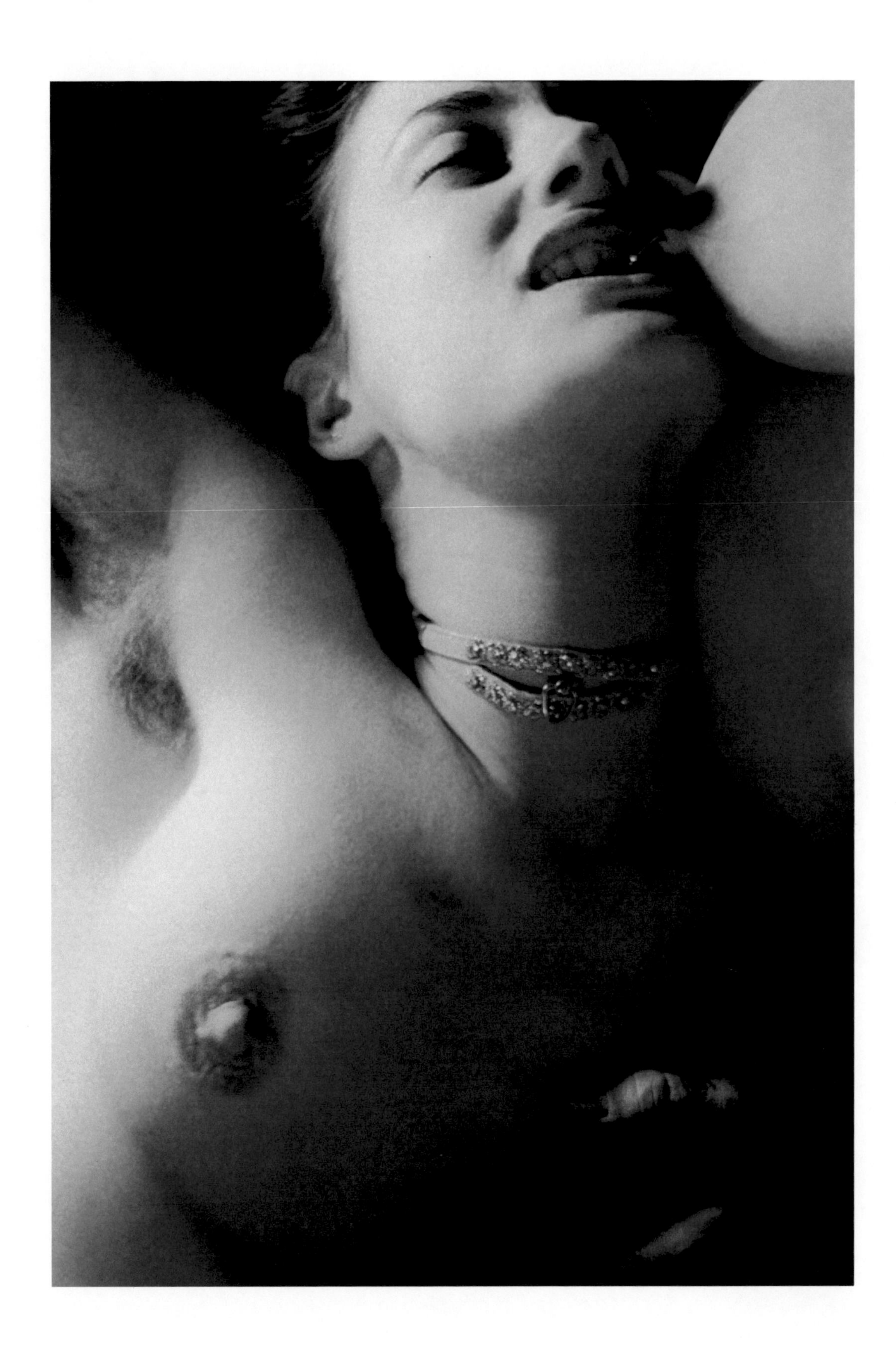

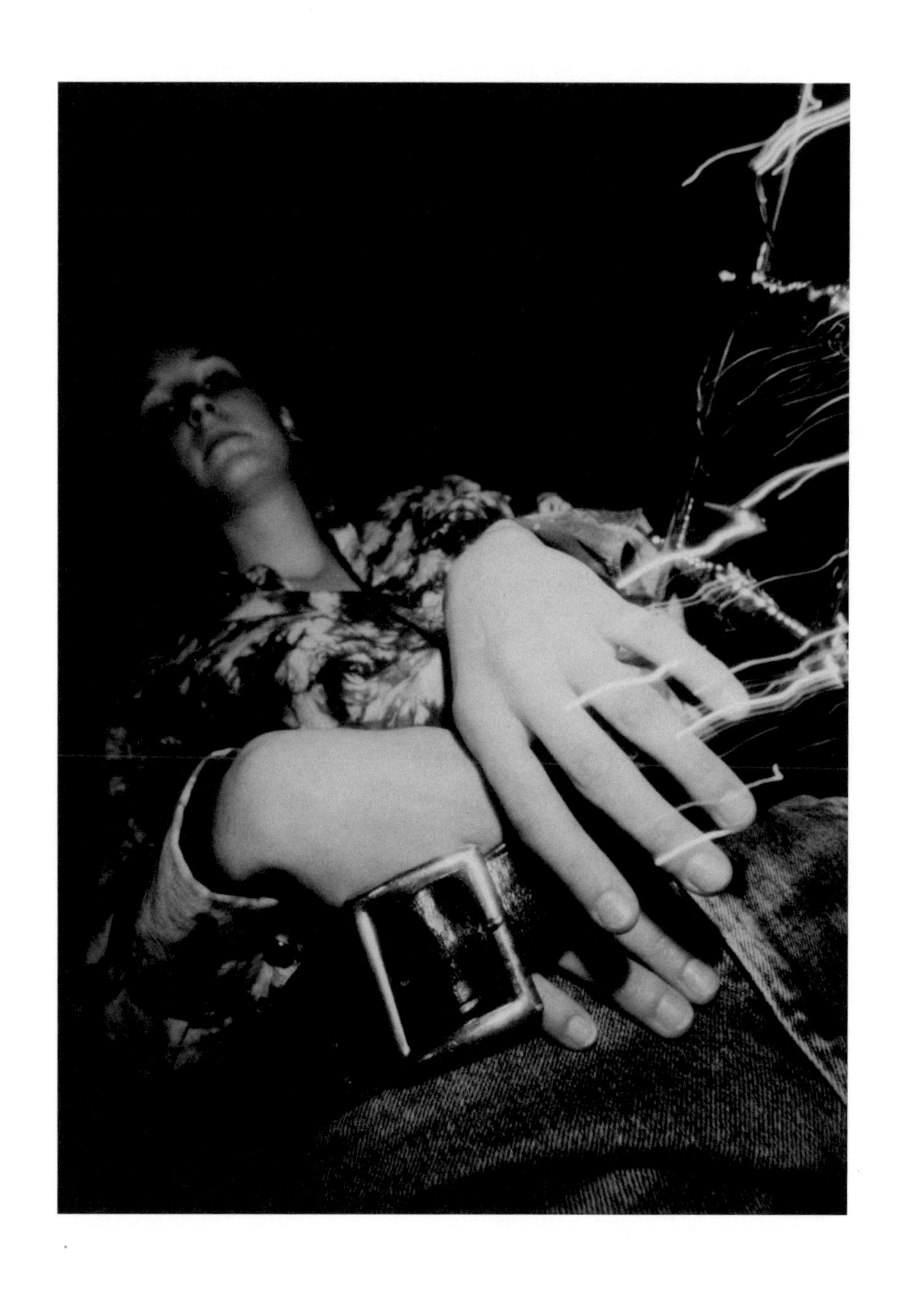

Do Lesbians cruise hands?

Fatter
than Barbie
Butcher
Than Ken

QUEER
NATION
QUEER
NATIO

KISS

INTERSTATE
RENTALS
800 322-3536
INTERSTATE
RENTALS
800 322-3536
Boycott
Burroughs-
Wellcome
Stop
AIDS
Profiteering
Queers

"PRO-LIFE" IS A LIE
THEY DON'T CARE
IF WOMEN DIE

THE RELIGIOUS
RIGHT IS
DEAD WRONG

Abortion without Apology
We Won't Go Back!

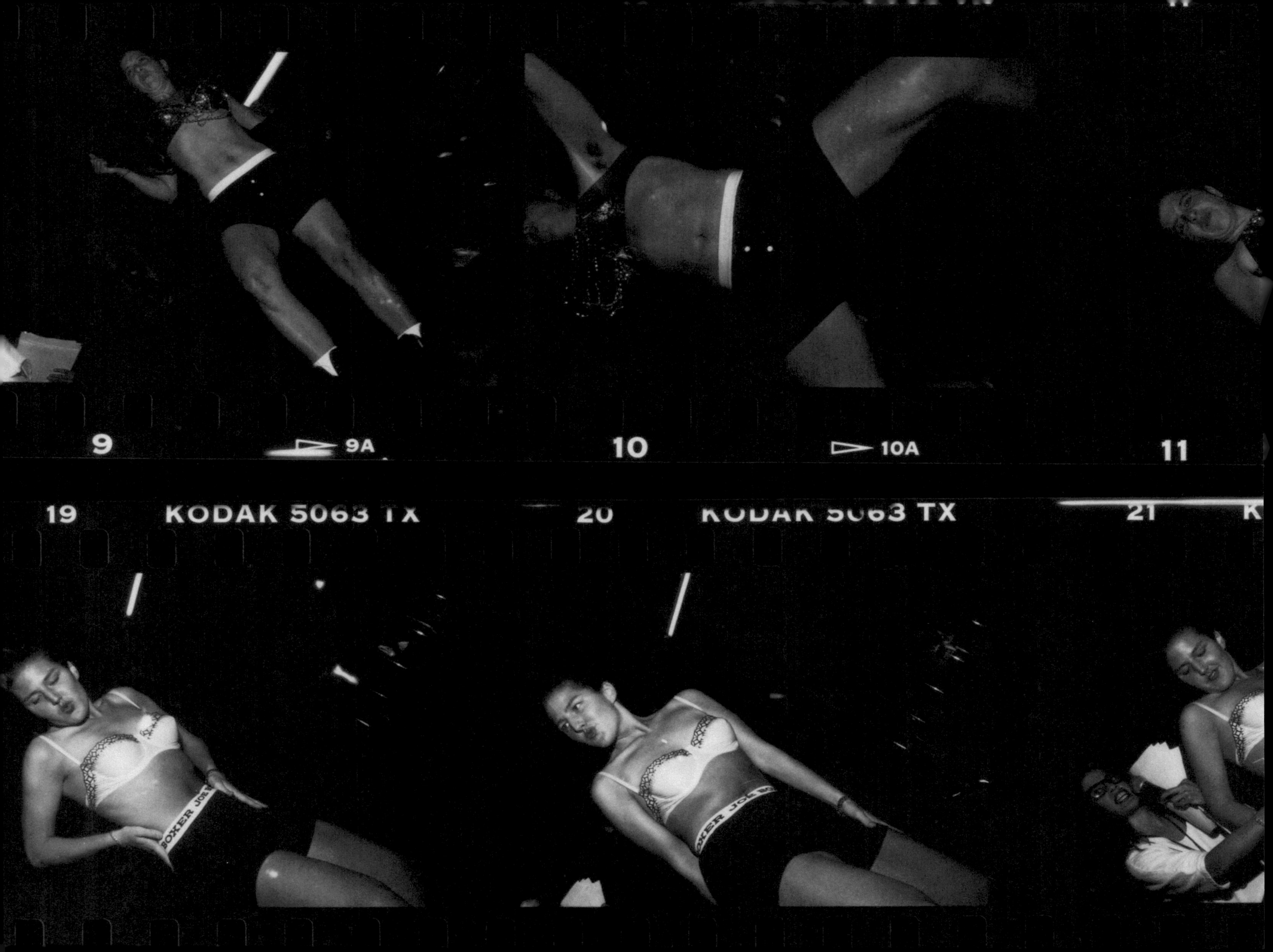
9
9A
10
10A
11
19
KODAK 5063 TX
20
21
BOXER JOE

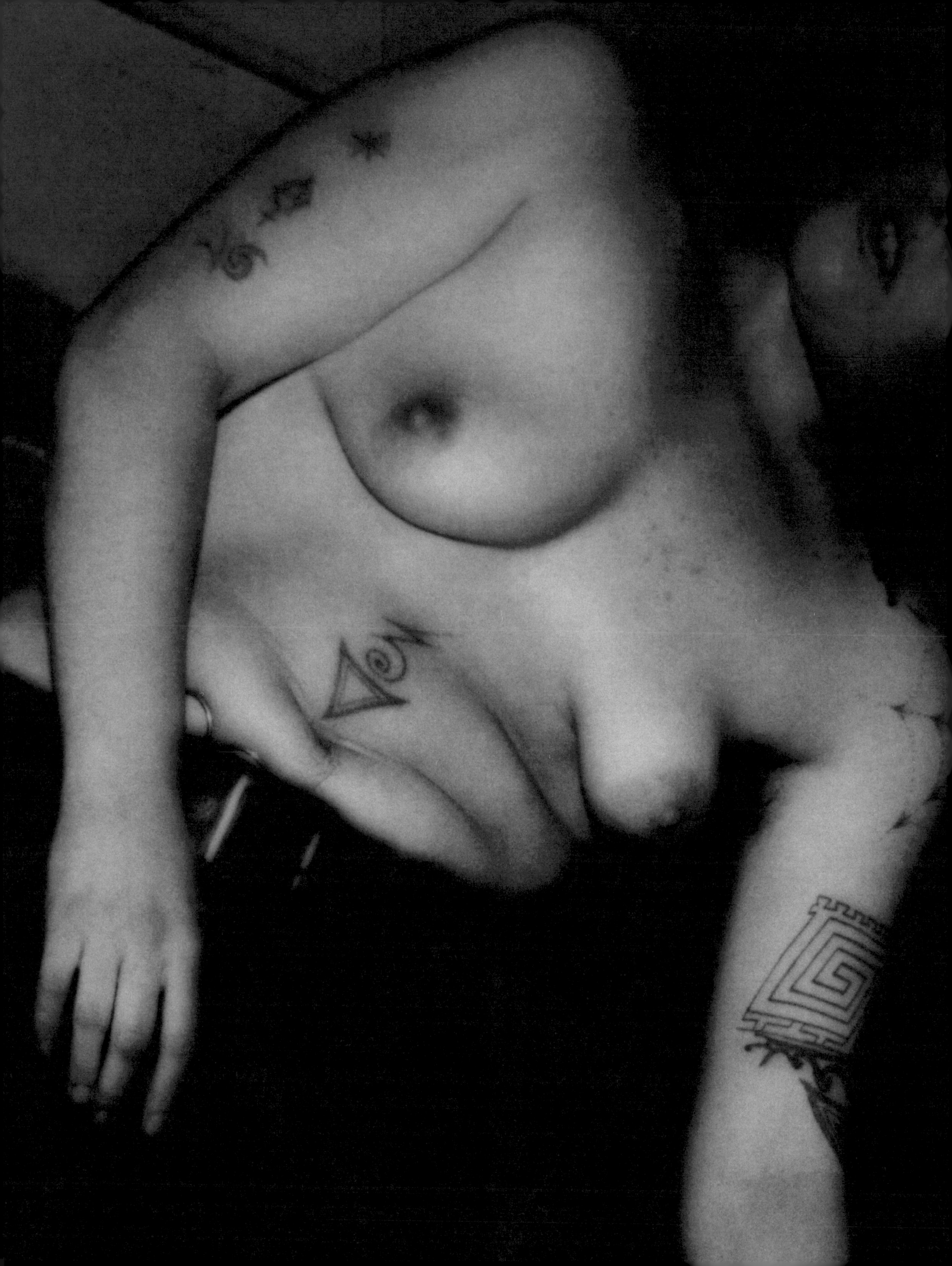

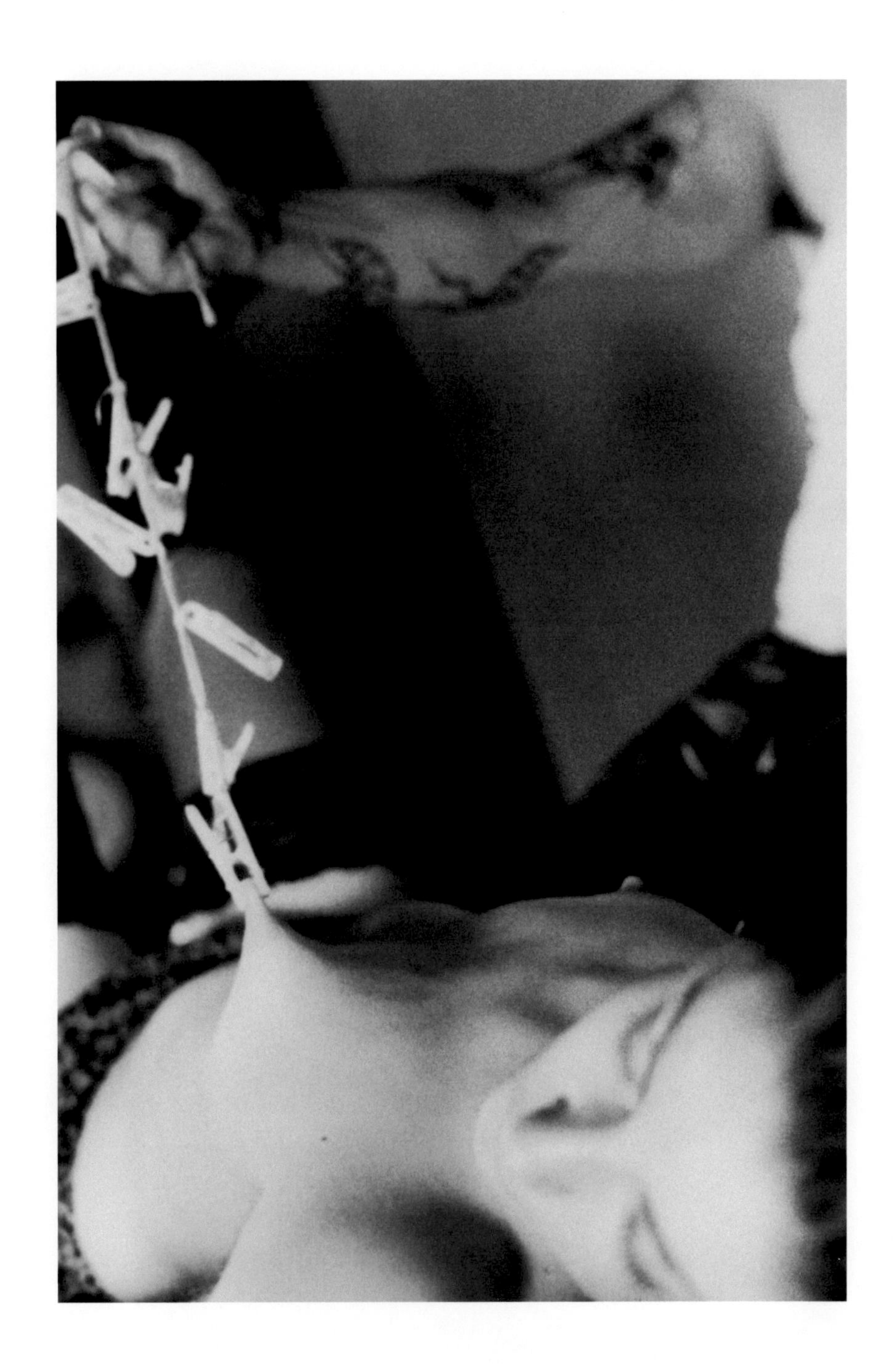

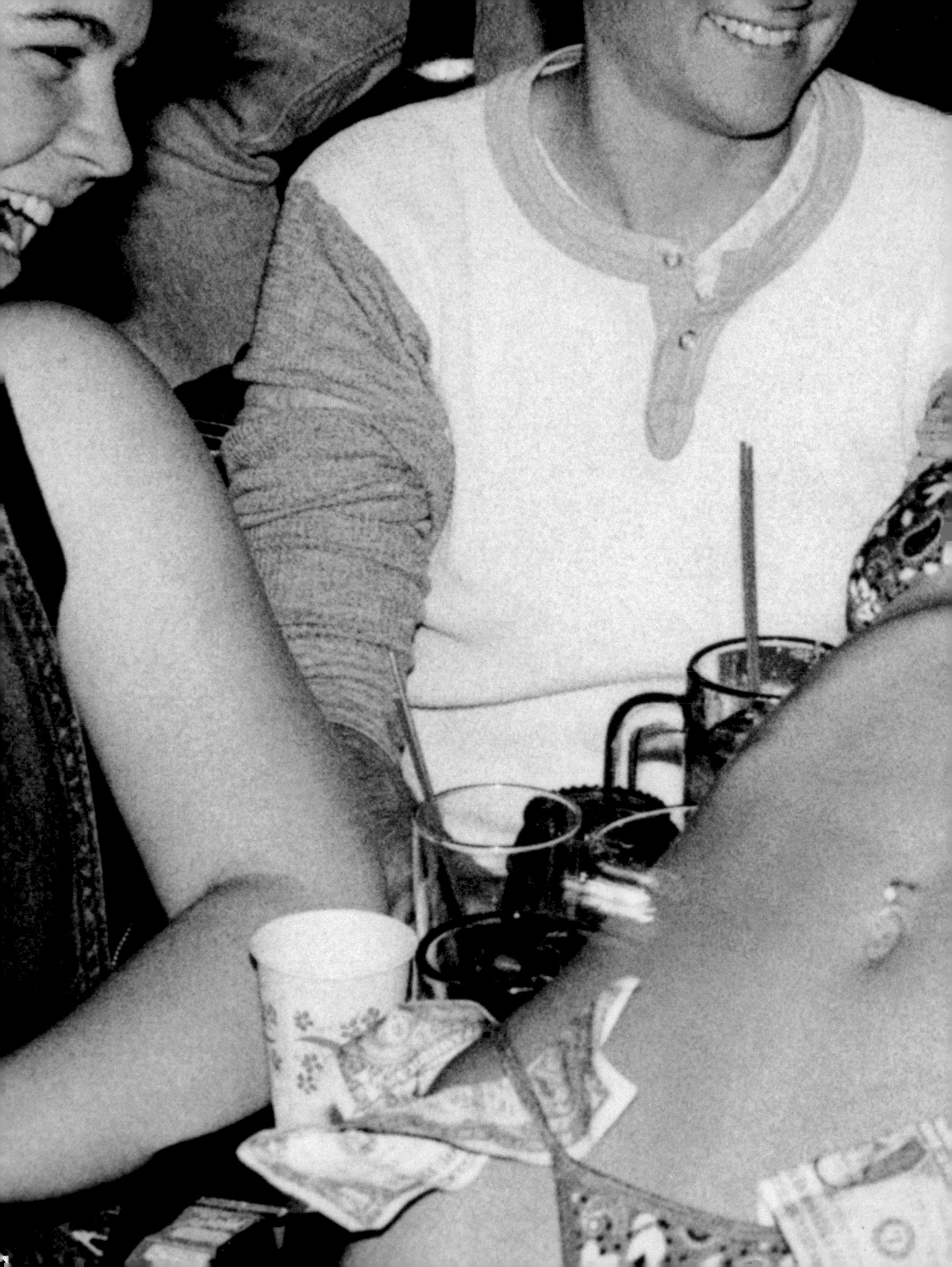

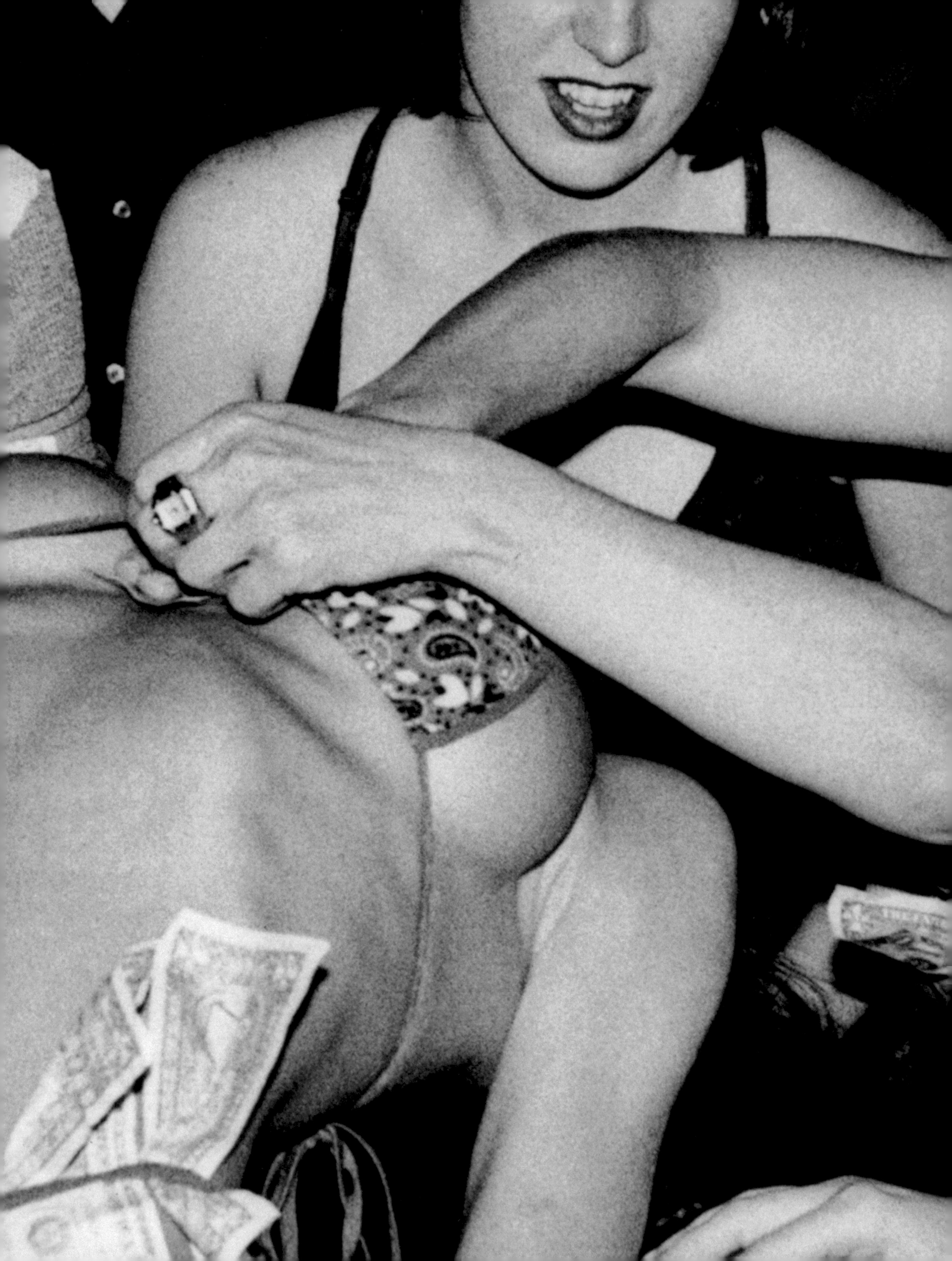

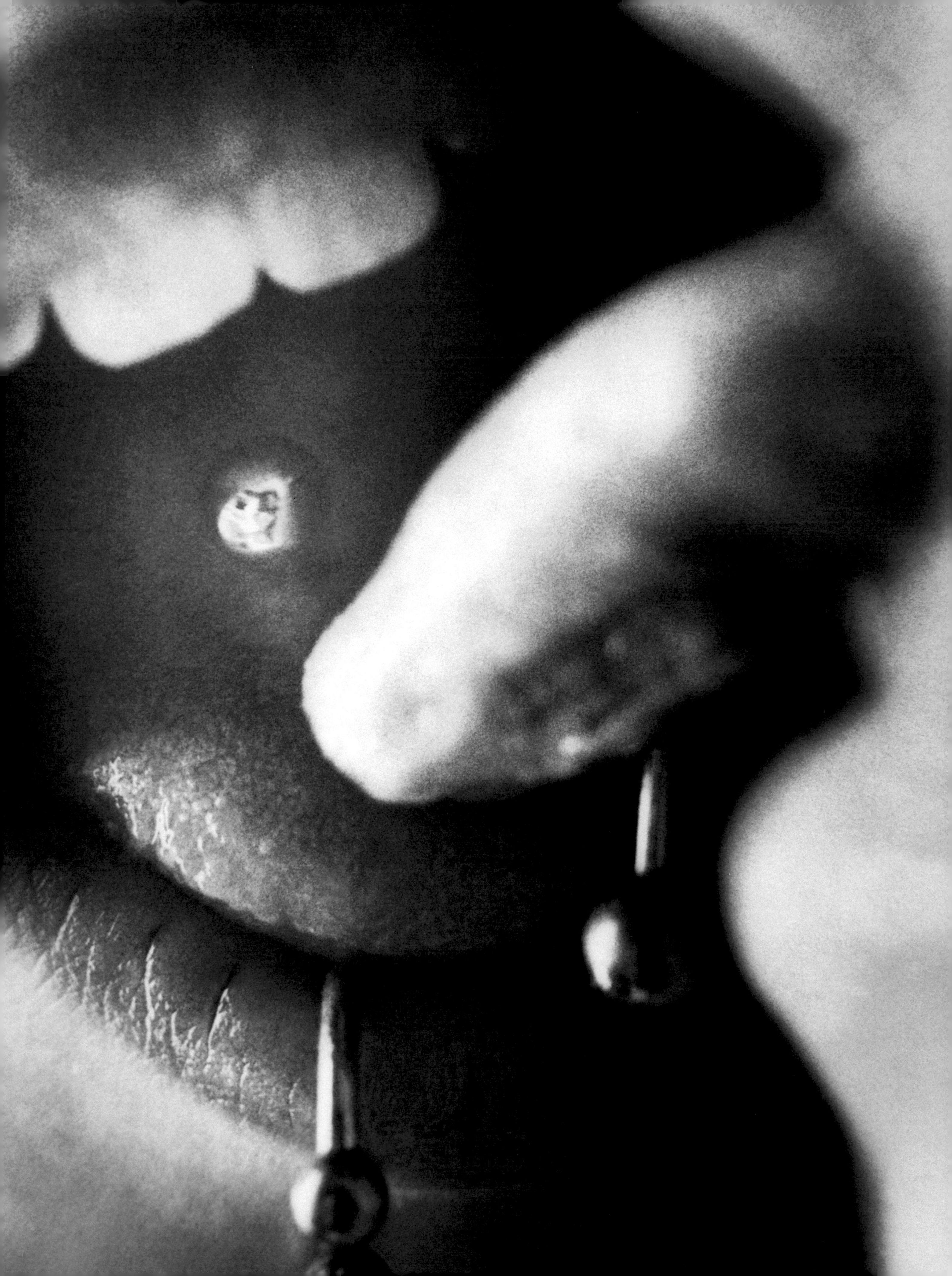

WINS
WINS

Daddy's
Boys

South of Market at Stormy Leather

Phyllis Christopher and Shar Rednour

Phyllis
As I remember, we met when I had my first show of erotic photos in San Francisco, south of Market at Stormy Leather, which was woman-run. It was Kathy Andrew who owned this amazing store of handmade leather fetish wear for women. They invited me to have my work on the wall, so that's where I put up some of my very early work. There were photos from a shoe fetish shoot that I had done with Lulu Belliveau at *On Our Backs* magazine. I think you had previously seen this photograph. And we hadn't met yet but all of a sudden, this beautiful blonde woman comes up and grabs me — I remember you grabbing me — and I thought, what a fun person! You said, 'I love that shoe photograph and I must have it someday! Who are you?' It was just such a natural friendship after that.

Shar
I actually remember where it was hanging — by the stairs, of all places. I think there was a staircase to an upstairs office.

Phyllis
It wasn't a real gallery. The work was probably dangling off a handrail.

Shar
The reason I came to Stormy Leather that night was that Mimi took me there on a date. We came from Susie Bright's reading, in the back of A Different Light bookstore; they had that beautiful garden there in the Castro, and then we carried on to your show. Mimi was wearing these cow pants, I'll never forget.

Phyllis
Were they chaps?

Shar
Yeah! Those black and white pants, remember those?

Mimi was opening for Susie's reading. She made a few jokes about femmes assuming all butches are stone butches and so never can get laid — with the femmes all being bottoms. And I raised my hand in the crowd and I said, 'Well,

you haven't met the right femmes yet.' She was super-queer-Mimi, she knew everybody in the city and what a good date she was for me as the I-know-nobody young femme. I really had a lot of *umpf* but I didn't know anything. So, she brought me that night. And when I saw that shoe fetish photo of yours... it would be the equivalent of when I first also realised I was gay! It was like a stiletto dagger — but not in a bad way, not killing me, but where you cut open your heart and lightning flies out of magic lightning glitter. It totally got me, right to my core. And I was like, oh my god! It just completely opened up everything to me. It unlocked a part of my brain that I didn't even know I had.

I was so poor then. I am not lying when I say I was living off free vodka drinks from my bartender friends and ramen. You remember I weighed 110 lbs, and I was volunteering at *On Our Backs*, and I was working at a preschool making pennies. So, I said to you, because I just had to have that picture, 'I will give you a dollar a week for the rest of your life, please just let me buy this somehow, some way!' And you said, 'Yes, we can work something out.' I think you might've only charged twenty-five dollars for it.

Phyllis
Oh, I hope I didn't charge you at all...

Shar
Right here behind where I'm sitting, I just realised, is one of your pictures, of me and my partner Jackie on top of me, holding me down. It's one of your later photos.

Phyllis
Ooh! Oh, I love that shoot. That was for the *Bay Guardian* when you won an award for your video. It just reminds me that there were so many women in San Francisco. You would tell them what your dream was, what your project was, and they would say, 'Oh, I know someone who likes that too, or could help you.' Before you knew it you were doing your project. It was a real place of 'Yes. Yes, yes.' I had been in communities where people were more negative or just thought things couldn't happen. But at that time, it was just like, 'Oh yeah, that's cool. Of course it can happen!'

Shar
One of the problems now, with San Francisco being so rich and millionaire-land, is that people don't have room to make mistakes and they *need* to have room to fuck up. With our generation in San Francisco and with our lesbian friends, you could go and have an art show and it could be a success or it could not be a success. Remember all the wild Klubstitute shows, and all the weird art installation shows, and the performance art?

I remember, before I moved to the city, the drag queens that I knew were the really glamorous ones in Chicago and Indiana; my ex-girlfriend and I would go to a really fancy drag show, and the drag queens were all perfect. In San Francisco some had moustaches! At first, I was like, 'Should I be offended by this?' And then thought, oh no, actually that's their expression. There was that one space called Build which was one of the places that really encapsulated that. To be able to be an artist, you need to screw it all up, do it right some of the times. There shouldn't be this pressure; 'Oh my god, if this show goes bad then I'll lose my place, I'll lose my rent, I'll lose my job.'

With like minds, and all the convergence we had, we were feeding off and really fuelling each other's ideas and projects. What we needed for our art — actual space and freedom — was also true for our sexuality. We wouldn't think anything about going up to the balcony of The Cafe or going over to El Rio or somewhere and meeting a stranger and saying, 'Oh, you're a bottom? Well, I'm a bottom. Oh, so-and-so does this, or they like a ball gag.' It wasn't some big deep secret, it didn't mean finding out the mystery of your soul. Some people might not find it fun to talk and experiment like that, maybe, I don't know, but for us it was so much fun.

Phyllis
It was really liberating for a very long time. I'm just thinking about the reason we did this work and how we felt coming out of the eighties. The government had been completely negligent regarding AIDS, we were in the middle of the crisis and since there was no proper education about how to prevent transmission, it became a life or death act to speak about sex, and to speak about it very graphically.

Our work was very motivated by wanting to explain safe sex but also to have a great time — it was a very dark period in which we needed our community and we needed a party.

Shar

I moved to San Francisco in June, so Gay Pride month, of 1990, and I'll never forget, one of the very first things I did was to go into the Castro and order ice cream bonbons at this epic, classic theatre. The LGBT film festival was playing, I literally had ninety-nine dollars to my name, so it was outrageous to put six into seeing a movie.

What's funny about me is when I first visited San Francisco, in 1988, I was joining this whole crowd of Beat writer enthusiasts and it went completely over my head initially that it was *the* gay area to be. I remember I had a lot of mixed feelings. I was coming from the Midwest, where there was a lot of misinformation about AIDS. It was the same for everybody in the mid-eighties, I think, but in some communities, with the lack of knowledge and resources, it was an even bigger problem, more pronounced. I don't know how it was for you in Buffalo, but I didn't really know about Harvey Milk. I'd heard his name somewhere, but it was in the back of my head.

I knew City Lights bookstore and about long ago, like 1950s and 1960s stuff. I didn't know about *On Our Backs*. On my very first birthday in San Francisco, in October of 1990, I was with eight gay men. I had zero lesbian friends. Obviously, AIDS was very much on my mind and I worried so much. At the same time, I felt that the younger generation was empowered, like 'we know how to wear condoms.' I was mostly worried about my older friends. But by older, I'm trying to think what that would even mean. When you're twenty-three, if somebody's just five years older they seem ancient to you.

Phyllis

San Francisco so gently turned me into a woman, I always felt. Because, you know, it wasn't too much fun to be a lesbian in a smaller town. The lesbian communities I experienced, generally speaking at that time, were either hard-drinking or really academic and serious and argumentative.

Shar
To the people who had been in San Francisco for a while, it was really, really sad. Nan Kinney and Debi Sundahl who co-founded the magazine said as much, as they were counting the bodies that went by in 1986, '87, '88... of their best friends who were gay men. When our generation showed up, it's hard to say, but I feel like we were almost an infusion to them. Like when you're just on your deathbed and they come in with the plasma and the antibodies, that was us for them.

Phyllis
I think it was the first time a lot of us felt empowered — to photograph one another, for one thing, without fear. It was at a time when you could move from your small homophobic town to San Francisco, change your name and do whatever the hell you wanted, knowing you wouldn't ever have to deal with those bullies at home again because you were just doing what you needed to do to grow in an encouraging environment.

Shar
It was our age of being sexual. The straight people had the 1960s, the gay men had their time of the bathhouses, and we arrived in the time of the lesbians. I think we had our personal release of not having to be in a dark bar and alcoholic in order to exist and live.

Phyllis
I've always liked how you've placed it in history because San Francisco is well-known first for the Beat generation, but then for the hippies and free love... I grew up reading about San Francisco and I was always curious, and by the end of the eighties it was definitely time for lesbians to party because we had just gone through so much sadness, at a very young age. I was in my young twenties when the AIDS crisis began.

Shar
We had taken care of people. We had watched some people die. I'm graduating from high school in 1984, so imagine, right when you're supposed to be becoming sexual, you're told that sex kills you.

It was during all the oppression, all of everything that was going down with Reagan weighing us down.

Phyllis
There was so little help, and way too late. LGBT rights were never on the agenda with the Republicans. Our community was openly ridiculed and the religious right claimed that AIDS was God's will. They were hoping it would just kill all of the gay men. Lesbians weren't even mentioned until the Clinton administration — remember when Roberta Achtenberg, who was one of the few out politicians, was nominated for a post by Bill Clinton and Jesse Helms, a Republican Senator, felt completely fine saying 'I won't vote for that woman because she's a damn lesbian'? We were just used to being disrespected — of course we did our best to re-appropriate the insult and everybody had T-shirts that said 'Damned Lesbian'.

My point is, you can look back from our current era, and think it's frivolous, but we thought of lesbian sex photography and writing about sex as a very political thing to do. Of course, just ten years ahead of us there was Tee Corinne and Honey Lee Cottrell and all these wonderful women who had started the whole genre. But we needed to continue it.

Shar
One of the things that you and I in particular absolutely loved were the fetishes. I got to really feel my own sexuality, feel it blossom, and investigate. I felt really happy that we could do whatever we wanted to with those fetishes and not be told, 'Hey, that's not sex. That doesn't belong in a sex magazine.' Because we were like, 'What is sex? What does that mean?' You know that painting of the curler in my mouth?

Phyllis
Yes, that Sarah-Joy Ford painted?

Shar
Does Sarah-Joy know that was us discussing what penetration means?

Phyllis
I told her about the issues the magazine faced

around censorship that prompted that whole photo spread. Anything that wasn't a penis was considered a 'foreign object' so was illegal to depict...

Shar
I think that's in the photo spread, 'What is penetration? Who defines it?' So, what did we do? I've got 1950s pink curlers on my fingers. It was a very camp way of saying... 'There are many ways to define penetration outside of the heterosexual model.' It was so fantastic.

Phyllis
Weren't we censored because you were tied up in Christmas lights?

Shar
That was another time, after the penetration issue, we were censored in the one with me photographed wearing Christmas tree lights, which they mistook for non-consensual bondage! That got stopped at the Canadian border.

Phyllis
There were absurd moments when we just innocently thought, 'Oh how cute! Let's do bondage in lights.'

Shar
I was a Christmas tree with presents underneath. And there was a subscription ad like, 'Subscribe, it's your present! Shar's your tree.'

Phyllis
You were this very pretty tree, wearing a lavender dildo, I might add, and obviously having a great time. And they censored it, suggesting you were tied up against your will.

Shar
Oh, those days!

Phyllis
You did have to know somebody... Feminist bookstores often wouldn't carry the magazine because they felt it was anti-woman and violence

against women. I think it got hidden behind the counter in some women's bookstores, you could maybe buy it in gay bookstores in New York City, as I remember. But I found *On Our Backs* through friends talking about it and then hunting it down.

Shar

What's funny was there was a women's bookstore, Dreams and Swords in Bloomington, Indiana, and it was actually a really good bookstore. I found my way there thanks to JoAnn Loulan, who was always so great because she could push people's boundaries as a comedian, but then she was safe to look at... She ended up being a therapist, you know? And I lived in one of those college towns where you wait all year long for the lesbian to go on tour, and JoAnn Loulan comes to town. She was making fun of the lesbians who were scared of dildos, but not so much that they wouldn't buy her tickets. And then she says, 'You can go to Dreams and Swords bookstore and this is going to be under the counter.'

So, I'm having sex with a girl and realise that this is not enough, I'm gonna run to where JoAnn Loulan said... so I throw open the doors at Dreams and Swords where normally I was just buying witch supplies, and I buy a dildo from them. Later I come back and say, 'Do you have anything that's like a *Playgirl* but for lesbians?' So, she goes, 'Well, just so you know, some people get really offended or don't like it or blah-blah-blah...' She reaches under the counter and pulls it out. And the first time I looked at *On Our Backs* was there, and I thought, oh, here are these ugly masculine lesbians in bad Wrangler jeans... at a glance I didn't think of anybody as sexy. I was going on my patriarchal raising. It was also pricey for me. So, I didn't buy it.

But then I come to San Francisco and I end up babysitting for Susie Bright. As a writer, I wanted to intern or volunteer somewhere, but I also just really wanted to work at a queer organisation. And even then, even in San Francisco, even if you went to *SF Weekly* or the *Bay Guardian*, it wasn't like, 'Come on down and write a bunch of lesbian material, lesbians!' They might not have been out-and-out prejudiced, but that wasn't going to happen for a writer. And so, I volunteered at *On Our Backs*. When I started, I was packing boxes and working

with Andrea, in the warehouse, which was really not a warehouse but a corner of the office. But I was being high femme wearing high heels and they were like, 'Okay, we need to do something else with you!' But I was like, 'I can pack a box in heels!'

Phyllis
It was a corner of the office, yeah. A very fun office. Coming from any other job to work for *On Our Backs* was just an amazing experience of being out, being able to say whatever you wanted about what you had done the night before. Today I tell people, that's what we did for ten years in San Francisco, we explored sex. We talked about it with all our friends, it was like our sport.

Shar
It was our conversation, everything we talked about. We compared notes.

Phyllis
We learned about ourselves in a wonderful, healthy way. And in the larger community there were always events in bars, very sexualised events, strip nights. You produced a boxer short contest one night; it was just delightful to say, 'I'm a lesbian. This is a lesbian night. And we're going to do something very lesbian, that no one's going to understand but we're lesbians because we love boxer shorts.'

Shar
We brainstormed it into existence. That's what we did with so much stuff. That's how you ended up with me on the edge of cliffs and afterwards you told me you were afraid of heights.

Phyllis
When we worked at the magazine, typically we went out at night, and maybe we had another job. I remember going out with you looking for models, frequently. We would have editorial meetings and think, 'Oh, who are we going to find to be in this photoshoot?' And you and I would go out with *On Our Backs* cards and go up to women — I was so shy but I forced myself to do it.

Shar
That was your demeanour when we would approach people… In a typical day, we would go into the office, we would have some kind of crazy meeting with Marcy.

Phyllis
We'd be hungover from a party the night before.

Shar
That's right. So, we're hungover, we come in with our dark sunglasses and we might have coffee and a doughnut or something. Susie had moved on so Marcy Sheiner was Editor-in-Chief at the time, we would be back in her corner; she had her gravelly New York accent and she just lived vicariously through us, she absolutely loved whatever story. We would sit there and put something on the editorial board. Then we would brainstorm whatever we needed to do. If we were going to go do some kind of shoot, sometimes we just walked down Castro Street and did a shoot. I remember sitting on a stranger's motorcycles for one, and for another I sat at a bus stop wearing my 'Nobody Knows I'm Gay' T-shirt, reading *On Our Backs*, next to an older gentleman.

And then we would go home and get ready. I lived with my hairdresser and I might get my big 'do on for Faster Pussycat. And Gerry might sew Barbie doll heads into my bouffant or flowers, then we'd go to the bar. I was the party starter; I could talk to anybody. You were very sweet and complimentary when you would approach people. I would say, 'Hey! We're doing this fun thing…'

Phyllis
Yeah, you would bring a jovial energy to it. One of the funniest stories is that over the years, we started just using the same backdrop in so many different shoots that it became a joke. There was this leopard-printed backdrop that got on book covers, got into photo shoots, and on and on and on. We were always doing this with no money, so we would just sort of scratch these photo shoots together. I remember making spotlights with paper bags. My photo equipment was just really…

Shar
Oh yeah! Sometimes we cut stencils out of paper bags for scrims.

Also, if we ever had a contest and I had to sign people up, it was actually just an excuse for me to talk to everybody. It was my way to work the room. Like at Faster Pussycat I could walk around the club and just say, 'Oh, do you want to sign up to this?' And whether they said yes or no, I'd be talking to every single person in the room.

Talking about the models though, is also making me think about that epic flannel shoot, which was one of your earlier shoots, and us piecemealing this group of people together. Amber, who was one of my friends from the Midwest, became part of that shoot. She and I had been in a beatnik literature class, and she was like, 'Why didn't you tell me you were gay?' And I was like, 'I didn't know, really, exactly.' And she was like, 'I'm bisexual.' And all of a sudden, she was my little bisexual baby I took care of, she was only eighteen years old. To this day I can never remember her last name but she was one of the three women with Elisa and Stephanie in that flannel shoot.

Phyllis
I remember how I met Stephanie because I was putting up posters for Karen Everett's *Framing Lesbian Fashion*, advertising for participants in the fashion show. We put up these posters in the Castro that said, 'Are you a flamboyant lesbian? Are you a tomboy? Would you like to fall into one of these categories and be in this movie?' And I put them up and I walked away and I could see Stephanie, who I didn't know yet, walk up the street. She looked at it and *laughed*. And I thought, she's coming to the show. She just loved it so much, I could just tell by her body language. And she did, she is in the movie.

Shar
Honestly, us exploring all the different angles — I'm grouping them together calling them fetishes — is it a sexual fetish or is it an identity or is it an exploration of identity? Is it an exploration of gender, too, or a safe way to play with that?

Phyllis

I think we were developing a lesbian visual language. We were developing a way to identify one another. We were like, 'Oh, why do you and I think flannel shirts are really sexy on some girls? Why are those boots particularly sexy?' And it really meant something to us. I think you and I took it very seriously. And so did Lulu, and a lot of friends. Maybe it didn't mean so much to other women, like they thought it was just fashion. But to me it was very important because it was the way we identified each other in crowds and in smaller cities. I thought flannel was very important to explore. Then we did the whole eyeglass photoshoot. And then we eroticised hands.

Shar

Which is epic for lesbians, epic. 'Creating our own visual language' — what you just said was mind blowing. That's really important.

Now you're making me think about how much, with my writing, I did obsess over glossaries and really weird words, always wanting to subvert, define, or put my twist — or our twist — on everything. I think part of it was about owning our own... like, if we lived on our own island that hadn't had the patriarchy, what would be our rules? What would be our language? What would be our twenty-four hours? What would be our nightlife?

Even Faster Pussycat was a part of that because I absolutely, completely, 100% am behind any sex worker and absolutely love and adore strippers, but just for myself I was always clearly aware — if we lived in Lesbian Land, I could be a stripper. But I never liked or needed money quite enough to be motivated to be a stripper for men. I actually had that whole idea when I was sitting there being poor, that's what I would think, I'm not that good of an actress. And then here at Faster Pussycat I could be a go-go dancer and have freedom and just wear crazy boots, go-go boots, and we could dress up in our vintage sixties outfits, and really be free.

Phyllis

We needed to figure out what we liked, because we didn't have a chance when we were teenagers

to date the way we wanted to, or to talk about what really made us happy or passionate. So, San Francisco was a place where my adolescence was explored. It was such a safe and wonderful place.

Shar

It was. San Francisco was a small enough city and in the artist enclave, we all hung out with each other so much that you weren't told, 'Only the glamourous drag queens are celebrated, no, you can't be a drag king.' You could be a drag king, or you could be a halfway drag — you *could be* a drag queen from here up, or king. We really borrowed and intermingled ideas from all kinds of queers — that was the melting pot of San Francisco — that we brainstormed and came up with stuff ourselves, and then we also, as a culture, were like, 'Hey, if that's good for the gay men, maybe that's good for us. They had a sex club, they had a bathhouse, what would our sex club look like?' And, 'Oh, gay men have different rooms, maybe we're going to have different themes... They will have glory holes at theirs, we will have a labyrinth at ours.' We made 'summer camp' a theme, we subverted the idea of the 'Wedding Night Bed' too — all in white lace and sheets. Remember that? We would take their idea and then put a twist on it, in addition to our own ideas. And that was really fun.

Phyllis

Gay male culture was a kind of template, definitely. The excess of their culture, especially in the seventies, was always what I wanted to experience. Then the protests brought us together. I remember it seemed like a couple of times a week there were protests. There were ACT UP protests, there were Queer Nation visibility protests, there was ACT UP at the opera, I remember that.

Shar

I don't know if you want to talk about this — but how about people being able to explore their sexuality because they were modelling for you? I remember shoots where somebody had always wanted to do a group make-out scene, or S/M, or fill in the blank, and many of them did it with us for the first time. We made their fantasies come true.

Phyllis
It was liberating for models — it was done for the pure joy and liberation of the women being photographed and for me, and for the lesbian audience who we assumed shared our desires.

The one thing about *On Our Backs*, was that models got paid, photographers got paid, writers got paid. It was very little, it wasn't the driving force, but it was always an important part of it. It covered expenses.

Shar
It bought you a cocktail after.

Phyllis
It bought you a cocktail after and it made you feel like you were compensated for your time a little bit. But the real reason everybody did this was to have an adventure and to feel better about their bodies and expressing their sexuality. Because no one had told anybody that they were beautiful or great before they moved to San Francisco. You wouldn't have had parents saying, 'I'm so glad you're a lesbian. You're so gorgeous. Go find the perfect woman for you.' We all came to San Francisco kind of broken and looking for a happier and more open life. The women who posed here were particularly brave. And I've always been amazed by that.

Shar
They were. You can't help but compare to the social media of today. For the people who always want to take their picture or put it out there, but now it's out there forever. When you're a young person you might want to explore... Back then, the women modelling for us could have this freedom of being really wild and crazy and out there, without immediate ramifications.

Phyllis
It was for a specific audience. You knew your community was going to see it. And your family probably wasn't going to see it. I've contacted as many people as I can who are in the book, even though everything's model released, but I wanted verbal permission again and I wanted everyone to feel great about being in the book. And everybody

included here has responded positively, and said, 'What fun — finally! — put me in the book!' Because the world has changed so much. The other thing we have to remember is that a lot of this work came before Madonna's *Sex* book, before sex was talked about in the mainstream media that much at all.

Shar
Tell me more about the stuff you noticed when all the young people started really blowing up around *On Our Backs* where you're living now in the UK.

Phyllis
Well, the first thing that comes to mind are my friends Janina Sabaliauskaite and Jade Sweeting, who were quite angry because they are both committed artists and were never taught about any of us at university. Honey Lee Cottrell... and Janina loves Tee Corinne — that first wave of lesbian erotic photographers were not mentioned during her photography degree and now people are looking back at this era and they are teaching it. I think we knew we were living through a very special time. But they were really angry that they hadn't known about all of these female photographers who are directly influencing their work now. Jade and Janina found out about *On Our Backs* at a gallery and were intrigued but couldn't find any more — they tracked me down and it turned out we all lived in Newcastle! This was in 2017 — they were inspired to create 'On Our Backs: An Archive', an exhibition at The NewBridge Project, which turned out to be quite popular and really re-energised my desire to put all of this work into a book.

In previous years, I had taken my work down from the web because it was getting used inappropriately all over the place. I was finding random photographs taken from shoots that out of context, lost their original intent. That's the main reason why I wanted a book; to put the work in its proper perspective, and to explain the political intention of the work.

Blood Orange

Michelle Tea

My first night in San Francisco, an army duffle as long as my body slumped in the corner of Peter's bedroom, his cages full of birds, winged dollops of colour, chirping alarm at my intrusion, we walked down the hill to the Castro. Peter's Noe Valley Victorian was lavender, but it sat above a bagel joint, which sort of killed the elegance. Proximity to freshly boiled salt bagels was appreciated, though. The house was high atop 24th Street, and we climbed a little higher then took a right down Castro Street, reddish neon burning in the distance like a faraway fire. The steep street had me landing hard on the ball of my feet, shod in those cloth Mary Janes you pull from bins in Chinatown. Blisters would come. So would everything else. I had warned Peter in advance about my appearance, emaciated from veganism and somatic stress and a general inability to take care of myself. Head shaved from gender problems. Thusly went my wardrobe, heaps of femme finery spread across the counter at an Arizona resale shop. 1950s girdles dyed pink, the garters dangling. The bra a matching bubble gum, sewn with rhinestones and pearls. A fuzzy zebra miniskirt with a matching cropped moto jacket. A black bondage skirt imported from London, the ass a cat's cradle of straps crisscrossing a gleaming zipper. *Come back, bring more*, the buyer implored. But that would require me to begin again as I had been, a queer, femme, goth, punk or whatever, wild, and then allow my gendered joy to be eaten away by patriarchy, sexual abuse, the sex industry, and second-wave lesbian feminism. A diet of literature by Mary Daly and Andrea Dworkin, plus *The Dreaded Comparison* and Animal Rights. How many threads of oppression could I tug from my life's weave, each string yanking another loose until I unravelled. I arrived on Peter's door in a pair of blameless 501s, far too big for my sculptural hips, knotted there with a hemp belt. My scrawny tits poked out the side of my too-big (don't call it a) wife beater, but if men didn't mind their nipples being seen then I, too, would have to not care. I was accustomed to existing under the scornful looks of strangers for years now, ever since taking up my vampire garb in the punishing environment of 1980s Boston. I was spit at in the street for hanging a crucifix around my neck; men hurled things out the windows of their whizzing cars: milk cartons, bottles, *faggot!* (But, I'm a girl — ?) If the spectacle of my peeping nipples became too much to live up to, or if I simply caught a chill with no meat on my bones, I covered myself with a scratchy wool flannel, green plaid and stained with paint. I thought this was how I would have to be. Gender-neutered. Shorn of all ornamental, expressive pleasures and their attendant, inevitable problems. I was trying to crawl back to some place of purity I had never occupied, beyond the brainwashing effects of a culture I had, frankly, loved. A culture of dressing up and transgressing, trash food, getting drunk, smoking, making out, getting spanked or tugged on a collar like a dog, books by and about people who had led scandalous lives. Music — sexy, ecstatic, euphoric music — made by damaged geniuses. Films gusted onto a movie screen, flickering larger than life in a wide, dark room. Life. It was as if I had died, or was placed in a dystopian re-education camp of my own doing. Everywhere I looked I saw misogyny, homophobia, racism. Classism, ableism, fatphobia. Systemic hate baked into everything from art to politics to fashion to social services. Language. I collapsed beneath it and wound up, after a meltdown in the desert, there at Peter's Victorian. Peter who had met me at my peak, fifteen years old, black lipstick cracking on my lips, a fake ID to buy everyone vodka, chasing goth boys I didn't understand were gay because there were no butch girls anywhere to help me understand that I was gay. Peter who I could always call and say I have nowhere to go and who would always say *Come here*.

Slowly, San Francisco returned me to myself. In the Castro, the hot lights of the theatre sizzling above my head, the city announced itself. All the men who hadn't died, all of them mourning or dying still, sitting in the windows of Twin Peaks, eating pancakes in the pleather booths of Orphan Andy's, buying Hot Cookies or porn from A Different Light or small, precious chocolates dusted with glitter from Faerie Queene. Coffee from the Cheesery, getting a shave and a hot towel at Louie's. Peter was beaming. He had been growing towards this his whole life. *The girls*, he told me, *they live in the Mission*.

Peter and I had grown up sneaking into gay bars. Jacques, in Boston's tucked-away Bay Village. At fifteen, it was the first queer bar I ever slid into. I drank a bottle of beer at a round, wooden table as a Queen lip-synched from the stage, full glitz against a backdrop of mylar streamers. Swiftly we were ejected, but often loitered around the spot at 2 a.m., watching the patrons disperse, the working girls and the chasers, the fags, the performers and the women who were not, actually, performing anything at all. We bummed smokes sometimes, sometimes handed them from our cardboard packs. We sipped the mixtures of fruit juice and booze we carried in our bags. I loved and emulated, strove toward an articulation of femininity I saw here, sparkle upon sparkle, everything huge, towering heels the foundation for a loud look rising to a crescendo of hair like the star at the top of a holiday tree. It was the '80s and a maximalist femininity reigned, be it the cresting bangs on the hairdos of the girls who fucked with me at high school, the tarantula sprawl of my own jet black tangles, or the metallic-iridescent-sequined-rhinestoned Queens commanding the stage at Jacques, working their glittered mouths around some diva's vocal howls or spitting their own nasty jokes into the mics between songs. If a Jacques Queen locked her eyes on you — when one locked her eyes on me — my blood ran cold and I quickly occupied myself with the puzzle of sliding a cigarette from my flip-top of Marlboro Lights. The *meanest* Queens, unlike the girls at school. I could not balm the wounds of their cruelty by assuring myself I was better than them — cooler, more worldly, superior. At Jacques, I was basic, easily eviscerated by an expert read of any number of Queens.

But no Kings. In San Francisco, Peter took me to a music venue on Market Street. It had a French name and inside was baroque as fuck. Gold gilded this and that, a swirling carpet, a chandelier? The stage had velvet curtains. And then it had Elvis Herselvis, the inverse of the Queens I had spent my high school years admiring and fearing. Donning the glitz of one of America's most tragic and glitzy *men* — Elvis, as campy in his emotionality as any tearful diva. Here was a *butch*. I hadn't known about butches, not as nouns nor as adjectives. Well, there was k.d. lang, I suppose. And that one dyke at the Fugazi show back in the desert, in a (don't call it a) wife beater and jeans, and my girlfriend had gazed her way and said, *Look at her it's like she wants to be a man*, her voice juicy with disgust, and I said, *Yeaaahhhh*, not really sure what to think, my head, as brainwashed with second-wave lesbian feminism as it had ever been with patriarchy, scanning the files for the appropriate theory to condemn this person's existence, and my *heart*, or some other pocket of longing in my body, reaching out to her in a shock of recognition. *I want that*. She vanished into the pit.

Elvis Herselvis swanned and sauntered and worked the room. He crooned and looked deeply into the eyes of all the femme lesbians, clustered at café tables, candles in bevelled glass shooting mood lighting up their cheekbones. His brocade lapels flashed. He approached my table. A metallic scarf draped across his neck, he removed it, and in a *flick* it was around my own. Peter gasped with delight. Elvis's eyes were so round, so wide and soulful, surely no one had ever looked so deeply into me, not such a sexy person, not while singing a song, not while a roomful of San Francisco queers looked on — *San Francisco Queers* — an actual *thing*, I would soon understand, a thing I would be part of, some sort of movement, a scene, a real scene, like London in the '70s or the East Village in the '80s, like the Beat Poets, or Paris in the '50s. I could smell the thickness of the pomade holding Elvis Herselvis's hair in its iconic pompadour. The floral shine of *Tres Florals*, soon I would use it as well, $1.99 at the Walgreens at 16th and Mission. As quickly as the shining scarf was around my neck I felt the soft tickle of Elvis sliding it away. It was a linger, the way his eyes stuck on mine, the slow drag of the cloth, stretching the moment like a slick piece of taffy, then, *pop*, he was on to the next table, the next girl made anxious by and for the spectacle of his attention. I slammed back into my seat as if dropped there. *Girl!* Peter said, his own eyes wide.

Something had happened, but it wasn't personal. And yet it kept happening, personally, to all of us, called as if by radar to San Francisco, to the dyke-glutted streets of the Mission. Even as each individual dyke made their own individual choices that catapulted them through the streets and through the days, the coldish, windyish days, the grafittied, dirtyish streets, dangerous and welcoming in equal measure. The same street you got the Dyke Solidarity Nod on one moment would see you gaybashed the next, and the two were inextricable. We were here, we were powerful, it was true. The city teemed with us, we had all responded to a thinly-pitched dog whistle which summoned us home, to find one another, to enact a brave and new drama upon one another's bodies. The violence was palpable and we expressed it through the sex we had, a place where one could safely submit to the hot, heavy power of being a victim, being sought and conquered, enduring it like a performance artist. It *was* performance art, perhaps all sex was/is. The power of being a menace, of bearing down so hard, of making someone take it. We lived with the paradox of being beaten, playing rape at night in delicious games that overwhelmed and felt necessarily primal, and then making our way home through the landmines of possible attack. Marya got jumped, two cars emptying out on her. Harry got gaybashed on 24th. Peter, clobbered in the head outside Valencia Gardens. That girl with her bleach-blonde hair shaved into a military fade, go-go boots and a pair of men's boxers, I watched her perform at the Bearded Lady, talking about the headfuck of *sitting on dick* all day at the Market Street Cinema and then spending her nights learning how to effectively beat the shit out of a man in a big foam suit. It didn't make sense, who we were. We were the living embodiments of some of the most degraded aspects of being female in the world. And we were sublime.

I was so sad the apartment I moved into did not have a roomy, iron, claw-footed tub like everyone else's apartments, but still I did magic as I soaked. I tore into blood oranges, a fruit I hadn't known existed, I squeezed their juice into my bath and sent the rinds sailing, ruddy little boats. I dusted cinnamon into the water. A Santeria store my new best friend, Heather, frequented held bins of scented bath salts. One was called Dream Boat and it smelled so good I thought I would pass out. I dug the metal scoop inside and almost cried as the scent wafted up. I shovelled it into a bag, tossed the bag in my purse, emptied it later into the bathwater. I prayed for love. I wanted to know about it. The concept of it. Sexy love. I prayed for sex. The power of it, for real. The streets of Mission felt clotted with it, thick as an exploded molasses factory, we were stuck in it, some of us were drowning, some would not make it. There was so little we could have, visible queers, *dykes*, in the '90s, there was truly so little of the world available to us, but we could have each other. We could gobble each other up. I was obsessed. With obsession. With the notion of it, the possibility of every stranger I glimpsed, and I glimpsed so many I had to close my eyes, to rest them against the glare.

Finally, I fell in love, it was requited, and together we set out to pierce our nipples. Everybody was poked full of holes, hung with metal. Cunts jangled like a neck full of dog tags. Making out with someone was like sucking on marbles. Clit hoods peeked coyly from behind lush labia, the silver catching the light of bedroom candles or bar top lighting, depending on where you were displaying your pussy. I watched someone, maybe Denise, lace her labia together atop the wooden bar at Muffdive at The Top, on Filmore in the Lower Haight. At The Stud I watched a metal skewer penetrate the soft cheek of a girl — if that's what she was — with ram horns etched into the sides of her skull. It traversed the hollow, dark space above her tongue and emerged, splitting the skin on the other side of her face. Every moment of every day felt like an occasion to be marked, imperative not to forget how it felt to be at this time, in this place that happened to be the dumping ground for queer sailors a million years ago and so now here we all were. The piercing clinic had sprung up around the sudden and intense Modern Primitive movement, as it was problematically — no? — called. *Mod Prim*, we made fun of it, me and my girlfriend, even as we signed up, to let a novice practice on us. This was how I had gotten haircuts, how I had gotten dental care. Fakir Musafar, whose photos I had seen in the *Modern Primitives* book, elegantly holding a cigarette, his waist disciplined into a sliver of the waning moon, guided his student — an older woman, as I was twenty-two, and so all women were older — to mark dots on the pink jut of my right nipple. I could not afford the right *and* left, nor could my girlfriend, but we agreed: *We're not trying for symmetry. We're synching up with chaos.* I felt a searing, terrible pain. I did not enjoy pain as some of the tougher dykes claimed to. I enjoyed the psychodrama of being acted upon in a sexy and malicious way, but stark, physical pain was simply painful. *You stopped*, Fakir scolded. *I told you not to stop, and you stopped.* Somehow she got the ring through my nipple. Iridescent purple, titanium, right? The cheap option. During sex with someone the little ball eventually flew off. A deliberate wound is like a pet, it must be cared for, but for a moment I was bejewelled.

Seeing tits everywhere seemed to promise an extraordinary sex; if disrobing, part of the ritual of normal sex, was happening in public, what might happen in private? Lynnee Breedlove, chest bare at a Tribe 8 show, a dildo swaggering fatly from the fly of his leather pants, a bowie knife wrapped in his fist, about to slice it off. Good thing all the dykes worked at the dildo warehouse, providing an endless stream of free dildos to raffle off or give away or castrate in a moment of queer, punk performance art.

I took my shirt off to paint the back walls of the Bearded Lady. Silas offered pizza, beer, to anyone who wanted to help. I think I was naked in a pair of vegan, pleather combat-style boots from Payless, painting the walls blue and eventually fighting with my girlfriend in the doorway out front on 14th Street. Normally sensitive, I grew more so when drunk, loved to roam the crystal caves of my emotions but it always ended a real nightmare. Why get so naked to paint a café, though? The revelation that one could, and the ones who gave the least amount of fucks ruled the day. Random displays of lawlessness confirmed that the rules did not apply to us. Literally they did not, as we were forced to break them regularly for survival, as queers, as sex workers, as drug enthusiasts. Our shirts came off at obvious spots like the Dyke March where our power was flexed so hard no one would step in to make us cover up, to cuff us and drag us to jail like had happened in the desert. I took my shirt off while dancing, too, because it was hot, and this was fine at The Stud, of course, but I was kicked out of The Café San Marcos, a badge of fucking honour to be ejected from that trash can, and again at some warehouse party where a million speedy fags danced topless all around me. When a culture insists you are wrong in a severe and basic way you are inspired to look at all the other blameless things the culture villainises and what is closer and more on point than our actual bodies, source of our queerness, so while we're tearing shit down let's get naked. After I was ejected from The Café I sat, still sweaty from the tight crowd, on a bench outside a coffee shop on 18th. A couple of older fags walked by across the street, stark naked, holding hands.

Sex just held so many mysteries, especially the esoteric sex I knew everyone was having, knew because they were basically having it in my face at nightclubs and play parties, broadcasting it with colour-coded tufts of cloth springing from their back pockets, and of course dykes had brought me home, pulled a knife on me or urged my fist up their cunt, not often enough but it had happened, and it felt like a yellow brick road that would lead me to something tremendous if I could just find the path and stay on it. My girlfriend who I loved so hard, I left her lying in my bed while I went and shaved my pussy in the shower. It took forever. Pubes clotted the drain. I brought it back to show her, *ta da*, and she was passed out, asleep. I didn't know that it had the plump glow of an *On Our Backs* model, anyway. I feared it looked plucked and rude. When my girlfriend teasingly referred to herself as *Daddy* I felt a sharp thrill wrack my body, but she was only kidding. Making fun of, actually, the leather-capped Dykes daddying around town. It was easy to laugh at, the intensity of everyone's sexual personas being performed nightly wherever dykes gathered. The seriousness of butch or femme, top or bottom. Wearing a black leather collar with a wide, silver ring, I was asked who I belonged to. *No one*, I'd said confused. I'd been wearing collars since I was a teenager, purchased from punk shops and pet stores. I was told that if I wore it, people would think I'd been claimed. I felt irritated at this

new code getting in the way of my fashion, but I stopped wearing the collar. I did so hope someone would claim me in such a way.

People would write papers about us, people were considering theories about the way we lived, but we were living on instinct. We had nothing to lose. We had escaped our horrible families. We had found new families in the streets, in the bars and coffee shops. We were redefining everything. I walked into the bar and the first thing I saw was a bare ass getting whapped. *I love crazy women*, a dyke proclaimed, and everyone agreed, we all loved crazy women, we all were crazy women, and for a moment we held that particular wild joy, until it made way for other joys, for not all of us were women, as it happened, and not all of our crazy would stand the test of time, would age well, some of our crazy would get us sick, get us killed, a lot of this crazy would need to be reckoned with, healed, managed, kept alight in us like an eternal flame that flickers endlessly at a shrine, devotees making sure it doesn't set the place on fire and never, ever goes out.

Meeting Phyllis Christopher

Susie Bright

I sleep under one of Phyllis Christopher's framed photographs. I sleep on a 200-year-old iron bed frame, a four-poster in a 150-year-old house in northern coastal California. You could say I sleep with a multitude of hauntings and Phyllis, a dear friend for decades, is one of them. She sets my nights and days.

Her image above my head is a bright and dark diptych of a lotus flower: a slick wet pod about to burst, and its dark underside. It's an arresting thing of beauty who does not feint to enter my dreams.

Phyllis is known for shooting a different kind of natural world — the suspense and beauty of unruly women. Her signal has not been pastoral. My bedside oracle, this golden lily, is a dyke talisman. It reminds me, in its tender wick and deep pools, of the first time I met her.

I don't remember the day the two of us met in the flesh; I remember the first time 'in the envelope.' Phyllis shipped me a package of her photographic prints under a pseudonym; I remember the colour of that day, when I ripped it open. San Francisco blue.

I was picking up the mail, because I was the editor of *On Our Backs*, a *fin-de-siècle* erotic magazine for the lesbian intelligentsia — and anyone else who could get a clue. It was, as it turned out, the first glossy magazine for lesbians about anything at all. We used to say in our adverts: 'The most intelligent magazine about sex happens to made by lesbians.'

A love poem brought me to the magazine. I was twenty-five. I did a poetry reading at Modern Times, a gay Marxist bookshop close to my apartment. A few days after I found in my mailbox a letter from a young woman named Myrna Elana, who'd loved one of my erotic outbursts. She was the co-founder of a new magazine in the works, called *On Our Backs*. That made me burst out laughing — I immediately got the joke. Topping from the bottom! She said she'd love to meet me. I didn't have a phone number for her, just an address in the Haight-Ashbury neighbourhood. I walked there from the 33 Muni bus with a handwritten letter that I planned to slip under the door. I wrote to Myrna that I could do most anything involving putting a magazine out. My phone rang that night. We were off to the races.

Our tribe was more devoted to photography than any *Playboy* editor. We were determined to show what dykes looked like, when they weren't pleasing anyone but themselves. We were not what I described as the *Cat Fancy* breed of girlie mag, with pictures of mewling models playing at sapphic romps for a male collector. Such images were the entire history of quote-unquote 'girl/girl erotica' — a charade for men who took up a fantasy, a hobby.

When you set out to create a visual world that has never been viewed in print before — by its subjects or seekers — you look for artists who eschew the mainstream options. That was what lesbian meant to us. We were a fast-moving, aggressive, anti-authoritarian cell, the way we had to be in order to survive. No wonder we coincided with the punk rock maelstrom.

On Our Backs published women artists, who lived or had grown up in places where the risk of criminal penalties accompanied what we did. We were the rarest: women photographers and editors. We were gay. We shot models whose autobiography was written in their erotic appetite. We revelled in the history of the great surrealists and anarchists who'd lived before our time, but to be honest, I think they would have killed to be us for a day.

Our payment was glory, the very definition of perverse self-satisfaction. We knew what it took to make a mark. Innovation happened in our demi-monde. We created it. You got only a few bucks for groceries and wine. *On Our Backs* was loved by outlaw women, who were not remunerated by 'the man.' Capital did not favour a lesbian endeavour — to the point where we couldn't get fire insurance, or a credit card account — 'because of the nature of your business,' the bank said. This was the gay-owned bank in the gay Castro district of San Francisco. Female entrepreneurs and artists faced ruin without a rational way out. The women who started the magazine came from working class backgrounds. There were no trust fund babies in our early years.

Before I met Phyllis, before the fateful day I opened her brown paper wrapper, *On Our Backs* relied on a couple of mainstay photographers. We were blessed by the efforts of a few baby boomer photographers who had been trained in art school and/or political firefights to within an inch of their sanity. Artists like Tee Corinne, Honey Lee Cottrell,

Morgan Gwenwald, and Jill Posener, were among the first to put the needle down on a woman-identified photographic image. Their pictures, particularly their nudes and erotic portraits, created the aesthetic mainframe for post-Stonewall lesbians. Although they battled for recognition in the chauvinist set, they'd escaped that cage. They took their considerable aesthetic gifts to the burgeoning 1970s lesbian feminist community. In those days, lesbian feminist printing presses flourished. We never thought they'd end.

Because of their professional background, I treated our first photographers as rudely as a newspaper editor: 'I need THIS, and I need it STAT.' *On Our Backs* had stories from our readers pouring in every day, and we needed their *visual* counterpart. We sought multi-page pictorials that mirrored our world — this took drive and ceaseless hunting through the terrain of women's taboo. Our first cadre had the appetite.

***On Our Backs*' other photographic contributors were our 'amateurs,' the women who sent us snapshots over the transom. Remember, this is pre-internet. Fans sent us pictures they took with their Brownies, their Polaroids, their first Nikons — and developed themselves. You'd never risk getting busted for 'being gay' at a small-town drugstore developer.**

I'd pick up these packages from our post office delivery box, and open each one with hope and hesitation. We had submissions from rural Indiana and Louisiana bayous, Odessa brothels, London squats, and Texas border towns. I will never get over that somehow they found us, they found the dyke erotic oasis. Even if the amateurs' photos were flat, devoid of proper light, out of focus... I would beg Honey Lee, our first staff photographer, 'If we get their negs, can you please FIX them?' She felt the same as I: these women had taken the chance to be seen, to be true, and what they revealed had never been viewed before. So what did fixing entail? Devoted elevation: giving amateurs (lovers) the attention and production value they deserved.

One day I picked up a brown padded envelope with handwritten return address: 'Buffalo, New York.' Beautiful writing, careful ink.

For me, a San Franciscan to my bones, the sleeve was an intrigue before I even slit the cover.

'Is Buffalo, like... Niagara Falls?' I asked the postal clerk, as if he would know.

'Canada,' he said, which seemed to prove the provenance was entirely off the grid.

'How does someone in Buffalo know about *On Our Backs*?' I wondered. I didn't let myself open the envelope in the car. I could tell from holding it in my hand, that it had the weight of more than one print, and was packed by someone expert in protecting their work. The pen on the return address looked so deliberate, as if someone had... made a fateful decision. The sender's name was darkly romantic: Christine Vilm. Who is *Christine Vilm*? I had never heard of her.

I'm glad I was alone in the office when I opened the package. I was able to hold my breath, without interruption. This wasn't an amateur submission. Christine Vilm? She was an artist. The prints were exquisite. Their subject was explosive. There was a model, maybe one, maybe a second, shot in a state of violent, ecstatic, disarray. Their faces were hidden, common in our closeted era outside of San Francisco. But you would hardly describe them as 'holding back.'

In one image, a woman is body down, face pressed to the floor, her head adjacent to a bare lightbulb lolling on the same hard surface. It is as if both the woman and the ball of light had been torn asunder after a night of drinking and fucking.

The next photo was an anthem. You see a skewed portrait of a woman from her neck to her torso. Around her neck is a medium-gauge chain, like a bicycle chain, and a leather strap. She is naked, her breasts are low, free, and she is tattooed on her solar plexus with the emblem of 1970s feminism, a biological female sign. It's the kind of symbol I imagined when Helen Reddy sang, 'I am woman, hear me roar.'

But wait a minute — I'd never seen a *Ms.* magazine symbol next to the unmistakable signs of S/M paraphernalia.

This same lean, feminine physique sported hair between her breasts and under her arms. She was a dyke who'd clearly come out in the lesbian-feminist era, but left it at the punk stage door, the grateful repudiation of vanilla sexuality. This female figure was

wearing chains, leather, tattoo, and giving no shits.

It was freak, in all the best manner, a rebuttal of straight-girl coquettish convention. A taunt to the politically correct of the snoring left. Phyllis's lens was kinky and tender, fresh as new scent — *My Sin*, for the '90s. It was gender anarchy before that sweet chaos was codified, just as I would always see her work. She was a wilding.

There was more. In another photograph, we see a chaotic female figure from the back, again stripped to the waist. She is muscular, and another S/M-inflected signature winds around her bare neck. Her hair is shaved in the back, like a soldier. She is electric, and whether she's in the throes of ecstasy or a good fight, it's hard to tell.

All of these pictures were lit much like an altar: incandescent and blistering. High contrast. Lens manipulation. What was going on in Buffalo? I couldn't take it all in.

I wasn't an omnipotent editor at *On Our Backs*. I knew my partner, our publisher, would take one look at these avant-garde transgressions and say, 'No fucking way.' She yearned for happy, beautiful, girls making love and looking forward to gay white weddings and prosperity.

That isn't what you're going to find from artists. I knew we'd been touched by grace, hearing from this 'Christine,' this East Coast border angel — she was rude, defiant and bohemian, the first of a new generation we needed if we were going to grow.

We needed the new level; we were bored with ourselves, and with 'I am woman, hear me roar.' We were in love with our club life, but trapped in our milieu of San Francisco strippers and outlaws. The rest of the world might think we were beyond the pale, but on our planet, re-invention was crucial.

Honey Lee saw the same thing. 'This girl is trained,' she said. 'She sees things.' What a relief. We took a pause. This young artist had studied and was already showing her own mettle. She was not baked in California hippie Haight-Ashbury acid dreams. She was somehow more radical than the work we saw coming out of Manhattan. She had catholic tastes. How could that be?

Lucky for me, Christine's pseudonym gave way. I had faced this curtain before, and with Ms. Vilm's phone number on the submission, I was eager to call. A shy and gracious Phyllis answered, only five years younger than me. She said she wanted to use a pen name because her family in Buffalo could not survive the exposure.

I said, 'Look, we don't insist on real names. You don't have to explain.' At the time, a son or daughter outed as gay, anywhere in America, could result in violent, life-ending retaliation. We all knew that. We All Knew That.

'But,' I went on, 'Your work is incredible. I don't know anything about you, except these few photos and they're over the top! If you don't use your own name, you can't claim the credit, and your credit is worth something. Change your name to live in public. Imagine if Robert Mapplethorpe called himself John Doe. You have to claim your aesthetic when you're an original.'

And that's how I met Phyllis Christopher, how she came into our lives. She moved to California, all by herself, which I only now understand, was a courageous leap of faith. She brought her dark bottomless eyes and tender love for women to our city, and our little Barbary Coast tilted on its orbit.

I never said to Phyllis: 'That was the luckiest day of our lives, the day you moved here.' I want to, now.

Once Phyll arrived in the City, as we call San Francisco, it was a full dive. We wooed her with compliments and introductions to an array of willing, libidinous, outspoken models, the likes of which lived exclusively in our homosexual paradise. The City was the place where you ran away to join the circus, and it was a three-ring bohemia. Our queer neighbourhoods were magnets for women who wore sex on their sleeve, their trespasses, their moxie. You could shoot every day of the week if you wanted to.

I didn't ask Phyllis what she was doing to support herself, but I assumed it was a day job and frantic freelancing, like myself. None of us liked to dwell on what we had to do for a living. *On Our Backs,* our social and artistic world, was everything.

I can't stress enough — the artists I worked with at *OOB* were as educated, experienced, and aesthetically astute as any man working in the *galleria* or the photojournalism trenches. But women had little to no chance of being recognised in those streams.

The professional photography world at that time was gender-segregated. Women could get jobs in print labs, doing black and white and colour work, printing for the male stars. It was as rigid as a construction site — worse. I knew more female carpenters than professional photographers. Look at who was being published by newspapers and magazines at the time! It tells the story. Legends like Ruth Bernhardt or Bernice Abbott were closeted lesbians and their exception proved the rule. Their disavowal of their sexuality was essential to their quixotic ability to be 'the one' among a male milieu. There was never a straight woman in their midst. That kind of femininity was insupportable.

Despite this fiendish environment, I got the feeling that... well, I *know* it... we were having fun. What I adored about Phyllis, was to be unlocked in the possibilities of that three-letter word.

Her work was tribal, whether it was one figure in the screen, or a crowd. You always sensed, in a Christopher picture, that there was a girl gang tucked around the corner, in an alley, under a bridge. The back room was where it was all going down. She's giving us a glimpse, the torn hall pass. Phyllis had empathy for female characters on the loose, she gravitated to their groove. Yes, we were dying of oppression and AIDS and abandonment but no one *lived* like us.

I was born on the cusp of Generation X, but Phyllis was its genuine article. She wasn't like our older contributors who identified with the butch-femme dynamic of pre-Stonewall gay life, or its post-feminist reinvention. She respected it all, of course it touched her, but she wasn't defined by it. I could tell by the way she talked about her earlier school days in the feminist academic milieu, that she understood their arguments, but found them stultifying. You had a choice, she saw: you could mire yourself in contortions, trying to make a clean fit of sexuality, visibility and feminist politics, or you could act. ACT UP, in fact.

Our first conversations, when Christopher arrived, were about our childhood. She told me she was from an Italian Catholic family, and that she had liberated herself among the punk underground of public high school. Just to listen to Boy George sing 'Karma Chameleon' on the radio turned listening into following — a gay anthem and code. We had been alienated, and then we had *fucked* alienation, and good karma was on the other side.

I told her I was raised Irish Catholic; I knew the drill. I recognised, in every shoot she did for *On Our Backs*, that her sense of ritual, and the vicissitudes of sin — the risk of the liberated eye — were upon her. There is no more avant-garde bohemian than the freed Jesuit child. You cannot understand kink iconography without Catholics: you can't bathe in the beauty of ritual without the host. There is no key to fetish without the body of Christ, giving you the side-eye.

We came of age at a time when fashion photography had a more thrilling grasp of sexual danger than traditional erotic photography, the 'female nudes.' Helmut Newton could do more with a high-heel in *Vogue*, than most men's porn mags could do with a store of sex toys.

And we liked shoes, too. With Phyllis, theatrical props and unexpected locations were everything. We created culture out of queer flotsam. A fashion era came out of the San Francisco '90s underground, and Phyllis Christopher can claim a healthy share of the credit. She was not just a witness with a camera, she was an instigator. Our drag kings and louche queens were our royalty, our flannels and leathers were our furs. We were the improvisers. That was Phyll's domain. Her commune-smeared lipstick on the edge of a knife; her Mary as a tender angel with curls, pissing standing up in the street.

I owe Phyllis an apology. I left her in the lurch. She was the only artist capable to take over as photo editor when I left *On Our Backs* in 1991, eight years after I began. My departure was the result of a divorce between the warring parents of our magazine, our PTSD — what a breach it was. The younger, newer staff should never have been caught in our mess.

Phyllis was kind and thrilled enough at the time, to say it was an honour to take on the mantel. But with that honour came a lack of financial support and sanity. After the breakup, the magazine lost a third of its think tank, and Phyllis was the most experienced eye in our office. Without the rising next generation of editors like Lulu Belliveau and Shar Rednour — well, let's not contemplate it. Their trinity and artistic fuel was pure nitro.

Christopher's work in the following years pinned me to her star: persistence is the artistic value no original lives without. Phyllis Christopher prevailed because she created something bigger than herself; we all did — and if you held on to that tail, the tiger would ride.

The last time I saw Phyllis in the flesh, our last shared temptation over New Year 2007, was her San Francisco going-away party. She was moving to England. She was in love and her lover could not stay — Phyll followed her.

But did that stop our comrades from gnashing our teeth and rending our garments? No. It was so hard to lose our darling, our inspiration.

We had the ball to end all balls. It included a lesbian wet T-shirt contest in Phyllis's Potrero Hill Victorian flat, a tribute to our heroine on her way to the North. Our breasts were unbound, and so was every rule. You have not seen a 'beauty contest' until you witness dykes without inhibition. Phyllis plied me with a chocolate fountain — as if any further delicacies were needed. We had everything: the bubbles, our peals of laughter, our music, kissing strangers all night not knowing or caring if they were boy/girl or girl/boy. Only women's nectar and audacity could produce such karma. Phyllis drew karma right into her lens, her bottle, her fountain of eternal youth, her backbone of sheer rock. That envelope I ripped? It was the sacrament I needed.

the zone system — the management of different kinds of luminance in an image that emphasises the bright halo of light around the model in Phyllis's photograph, rendering each drop of piss jewel-like — and the magical alchemy by which the metallic compound of silver-based photographic paper is replaced and an image drenched in the golden liquid tone of sepia. The gay clubs in Brighton, where I live, are mainly commercial. There is a lesbian bar that we know of, but its sleek pink interior is at odds with the DIY ethic me and my friends are into. And anyway we usually don't get in. At the LGBT youth group we surf the web unsurveilled by teachers and parents. Do I come across the magazine through the youth group, or do I buy it from the gay and lesbian bookshop that is behind a supermarket carpark? Either way I stuff it hurriedly into a rucksack and read it cover-to-cover in the bedroom that I share with my sister. A gap between the wall and my bed keeps the secrets of my first encounters with lesbian photographs, and contains my clamorous feelings: surprise, embarrassment, interest and excitement.

Fifteen years exerts itself between then and the first afternoon I spend at the home Phyllis shares with her partner Kate Sweeney in Gateshead in the North East of England. Alongside boxes of magazines, club flyers, and printer's proofs of book jackets are photographs organised within plastic sheaths in large portfolios. These hand-printed images have been variously reproduced, displayed in community spaces or simply made for pleasure or posterity, perhaps both. On my computer, I keep a few snaps taken that day on my phone. The photograph of Terese on Ocean Beach that I remember from *DIVA*. A black and white portrait of two dykes, their entwined bodies spotted in a pool of light and the edges of the print neatly torn by hand to create a thin white border around the inky black of the image. Held carefully between my thumb and forefinger these prints are framed by a brightly coloured rug, signalling the domestic location of Phyllis's archive.

Being introduced to a person's work in their home is a distinctive, emotionally charged, contextually rich, experience. A photographic archive like Phyllis's, which has until recently only been publicly available through print media, presents different preservation issues to those that porn scholars have identified in relation to video. Whereas home video technologies represented increased opportunity for the production of queer pornographic material, Phyllis began to lean toward more sensual, erotic expression in her photography. At the same time, homophobic censorship laws impeded which sex acts could be depicted and shared in print, and cheap printing — necessitated by limited resources — greatly affected the quality of reproductions. The material conditions in which queer print is produced and circulates offers possibilities for politicised aesthetic forms but there are also limitations. Encountered in 'the flesh,' Phyllis's photographs, which she prints and tones herself at home or in community darkrooms, display her skill as a technician and reveal a queer contribution to a modern tradition. (Researching for this book, I learn that, as well as being used to tone photographs, sepia preserves the longevity of the print.) The images that I reproduce quickly with my phone that first day spent with Phyllis's archive are sensual and tactile, full of joy. They indicate my own proclivities, something we make a joke of. Here's a snap of my girlfriend Elsa reading from a 2001 edition of *On Our Backs* with the headline 'The Butches: Unzipped.' The photographs and objects that we encounter in this collection map a recent moment of lesbian history. Our encounters with this history also remap a set of relationships in the present.

That day, between stories, laughter, and numerous cups of tea, Phyllis describes to us how taking a picture of a girlfriend while in high school was like a 'premonition.' Phyllis went on to scrutinise her relationship to her own body, building confidence as she worked with photography while enrolled on a Fine Arts programme in Buffalo. Though she took classes in women's studies with feminist historian Elizabeth Lapovsky Kennedy, in which a popular question was 'is there a lesbian aesthetic?' this work was made in a context in which there wasn't 'much intimate exploration.' Feeling around without many precedents, one early photograph shows Phyllis prone on the floor, lit only by a lightbulb in the foreground. The safe light in a darkroom provides just enough light to see what you're doing with your hands. Then a friend, Karin, invited Phyllis to photograph her wearing a leather leash. Like the self-portrait, these images are attentive, closely cropped and, shot in an attic, domestic in scale. A small tattoo of a clenched fist raised within a Venus symbol, the sign associated with feminist struggle, forms a constellation with a nipple. The self-portraits and the collaboration with Karin became part of a series that Phyllis named *Nonsynchronist Nudes* (1985). As the title suggests, the series reflects an interest in formal experimentation, a photographer pushing herself to see differently as she investigated the possibilities of the camera to distort and resist conventional depictions of the female form.

Nonsynchronist Nudes signals a visual language that is out of sync. In analogue filmmaking, non-sync refers to the recording of image and sound separately. Phyllis's photographs are out of sync with a genre, the female nude, through which various cultural values and representational norms have historically been established. Being out of sync also aligns with experiences of queerness, characterising the way that this series was produced at a time of paucity, when access to queer public life was limited by living and making work outside of North America's urban centres. Even in a city like Buffalo, the lesbian feminist sexual cultures that were thriving elsewhere were only available to Phyllis through the pages of magazines. Alongside personals and advertisements for vibrators, *On Our Backs* regularly solicited creative contributions from its readers. Phyllis sent a selection of images to an address in San Francisco where they were picked up by editor Susie Bright and published under the title *Lights Out*. In the three-page feature, faces are obscured and Phyllis retains anonymity under the pen name Christine Vilm. The precarious conditions through which queer visibility can be achieved inscribe themselves into the visual languages of images and the terms of their appearance in print, rendering as inseparable politics and form.

The desire to make images that 'read as lesbian,' as Tee Corinne once said of her collaborations with Honey Lee Cottrell, was both informed by, and contributed to, heated feminist debates about the place of sex in politics. By the mid-1980s, when Phyllis was encountering feminist theory in college, a deep ideological rift threatened to cohere around issues like S/M, butch and femme, pornography and censorship. For some, pornography, even that made by and for lesbians, was always already exploitative, repeating the traumas of patriarchal violence. For others, anti-pornography perspectives were viewed as a new puritanism, dangerous for their implicit — sometimes explicit — ties with the perspectives of the political and Christian Right. The reality of the so-called feminist sex wars was far more complex than these stark oppositions imply. Phyllis remembers how amid these 'unforgiving' debates she 'wanted to be playful because the discussions were so serious.' When, following the path of many queers before her, Phyllis relocated to San Francisco, she met a sympathetic community of 'well-informed women who said "what the hell, we're going to have a good time.".'

Moving to the city in what Phyllis's collaborator Shar Rednour identifies as 'the time of the lesbians,' she felt that she had found her people. The first feature that Phyllis authored non-pseudonymously for *On Our Backs* appears in the September to October 1990 issue. The series is titled *The Shoe Box* and was co-created by Lulu Belliveau, then the magazine's contributing editor for photography. Lulu also appears in the shoot. Opening *The Shoe Box* is a model in simple black underwear. She removes the sock from another, revealing bare toes among a pile of highly polished Doc Martens and other footwear. They delve into a chest, don heels and brogues, and adjust clasps as a bondage scene unfolds — a lesbian Cinderella tale. Another pictorial, and Phyllis's second cover for *On Our Backs*, is a photostory made in collaboration with Leigh Crow or Elvis Herselvis, a butch lesbian impersonator dragging as the king. In the early 1990s, queer theory was developing a foothold in the academy and its advocates were beginning to theorise various aspects of lesbian culture, including the prevalence of kinging in that decade. In 1998 J. Jack Halberstam (who once had a column in *On Our Backs* dedicated to 'Clit Culture' whilst teaching lesbian and gay studies in San Diego) wrote in his ground-breaking study *Female Masculinity* that his own interest in archetypical constructions of white, American, masculinity went only as far as Elvis Herselvis. Herselvis is a camp parodic play of both masculine and feminine presentations of gender. Phyllis's photographs show him in a clinch with his own Priscilla, combing his quiff and daydreaming in a teenage bedroom replete with posters of Presley. 'So what does she think about Elvis being a lesbian?' the editor asks Crow. 'Well, I always thought Elvis was a little on the femme side,' she replies.

These early features prefigured what Phyllis and Shar would come to call 'lesbian fetishes.' Informed by practices historically aligned with gay men such as cruising, the two went about compiling a visual lexicon — a kind of lesbian semiotics — including shoes, boxer shorts, and hands. This undertaking expanded upon a longer history of coded signifiers through which queers have announced ourselves to one another within the limitations and assumptions of compulsory heterosexuality. For lesbians, this has sometimes meant expropriating signs and symbols from gay male sexual cultures that have typically had more public means of articulation. In the late 1970s, Samois produced a lesbian hanky code. Designed as a folded card that could slip, like a handkerchief, into a pocket, and featuring an illustration of a bare-chested denim-clad dyke with her hand on her hip, the card decodes lavender for group sex, maroon for menstruation and white lace for Victorian scenes. The pamphlet explains 'it is often difficult for S/M lesbians to identify themselves to one another. Women in Samois thought the gay male style of wearing a bandana in one pocket or the other was handy, but didn't wish to adopt their code without alterations.' A similar ethos underpinned Phyllis and Shar's exploration of lesbian fetishes, though these extended beyond S/M. Their playful pursuit of (for?) an aesthetic language that spoke of specifically lesbian desires also generated performative articulations of dyke identities at a time when queer emerged as a political declarative in the late 1980s and early 1990s.

The queer lesbian. I think a desire for such a difference draws a new generation back to this recent history of feminist visual culture. The political and sexual proclivities of another moment appear in the present, at a time when lesbian identity is regularly instrumentalised, and not just by lesbians, in attacks on trans women's rights to self-determination and bodily autonomy. Then, as now, 'lesbian' is a contested territory. It is by turns, a strategic category for political advocacy, a convenient description of sexual orientation, and a lifeline. It has baggage, is shaped by on-going patterns of societal oppression and carries its own internal exclusions. At other times, it is not necessarily the right description for some who appear under its sign, historically, or at present, even in the pages of this book. Yet it is the sign that drew the community depicted here together, however precariously, as the terms 'lesbian' and 'queer' were each transforming the meaning of the other. To turn a phrase from José Esteban Muñoz, the photographs in this book are a residue of lesbians' queer evidence: they bear the trace of evidently *queer* lesbian subjectivities. The present interest shown by younger generations, including myself, in the work of Phyllis and her contemporaries, evidences that this history is as much a part of our political horizon as it is an artefact of a different time, a different place.

In summer 2018, Kate organises a screening of Karen Everett's 1991 film, *Framing Lesbian Fashion*, for an animated audience of friends at the Star and Shadow cinema, a community-run space in Newcastle, England. This 'educational primer in lesbian sensibilities,' as one reviewer wrote in *On Our Backs* at the time of the film's release, was co-produced by Phyllis. It casts a taxonomical gaze on the changing tastes and styles of lesbian community in the US from the androgynous appearance of lesbian feminism in the 1970s to the lipstick lesbianism associated with the early 1990s. It's a pleasure to watch, covering themes such as 'Cross-dressing and the butch/femme renaissance' and 'Fluorescent Fashion (Clearly Here and Queer)' as it assembles talking heads from the community alongside photographs, archive footage and recordings of club nights. The influence of Everett's film tutor, the filmmaker and poet Marlon Riggs, is tangible in the ethos of self-reflexivity that *Framing Lesbian Fashion* employs. Toward the end of the

film, we're delighted to see Phyllis and Karen don flannel shirts and ride with dykes on bikes at the gay freedom parade. 'My girlfriend and I decided to honour lesbian feminists,' Karen narrates as Phyllis is shown in a sleeveless plaid shirt fixing a sign that reads 'Flannel Forever' to the back of a motorcycle. 'This is our tribute to the seventies,' says Phyllis to camera as the chorus of Cris Williamson's lesbian feminist folk classic 'Waterfall,' released by Olivia Records in 1975, starts up. ('All things come spilling in on you / and you're flowing like a river.') Here is a form of 'temporal drag' a decade before Elizabeth Freeman came up with the term to describe a younger generation of dykes she observed wearing Birkenstocks and flirting with a style of lesbian feminism that had much to do with the 1970s and, seemingly, little to do with contemporary fashions. In terms that echo Phyllis's *Nonsynchronist Nudes*, Freeman describes temporal drag as an instance of queer asynchronicity in which a feminist past floods the queer present. Likewise, assimilating flannel into the present in which she 'can mix and match identities,' Karen advocates for the ongoing relevance of feminist politics despite contemporaneous narratives in the mainstream media that suggested its battles were anachronistic — that they had been fought and won.

Back in the archive, as I turn the pages of magazines and flip through manilla files with handwritten labels, it becomes possible to think of Phyllis's approach to photography as a manual process, materialising relations through tactile encounters. A photograph of Kris Kovick shows the cartoonist inking an illustration, a quickly sketched outline of a hand with 'Do Lesbians Cruise Hands?' written between the L shape created by index and thumb. Elsewhere in Phyllis's images hands are splayed or held, they cling and search. Sometimes hands grab and at other times they are in repose, relaxed. Hands are tender, pointing to a poetics of gesture through which queer relations are made. Behind each image, Phyllis's hand cradles a camera, finger on the shutter release. In her 2000 essay 'The Lesbian Hand,' Mandy Merck envisages a dialectical image, in which the hand is both organ, and product, of labour. Cruising films for the hand's appearance, she asks, if it is daunting for the male spectator (a sort of ten fingers better than one scenario?), what is its function for lesbian spectators? If all fetish derives from lack and fantasy, is the lesbian hand a fetish? Is it a phallus? Circling the work of theorists Teresa de Lauretis and Judith Butler, Merck comes to her own conclusions. Considering the promise of authentic lesbian sex in the Wachowskis' film *Bound* (1996), a promise potentially fulfillable because of the role played by Susie Bright as 'lesbian sex consultant' to the directors, Merck writes 'the hand can represent binding commitment, it also does so as an instrument of production, the process that materialises representations of sexuality and sexualities as representations.' In *Bound*, she argues, 'women get away with the money and the jewel of female desire. And they do so not by erotic conquest, but by a freely given love that binds each other — and that is made *by hand*.' The handmade lesbian culture to which Phyllis's images belong makes a similar promise that mainstream representations of lesbian sex do not; the erotics of her images are guided by an ethic of making (both photographs and love) that is relational and reflexive: *'Women meet me and say "will you photograph me?" I don't pay them. I'm honoured to do that.'*

Perhaps making an image 'read as lesbian' is as much about the set of relations realised in the act of making as it is the surface impressions and material products of that process. Histories of photography are interwoven with dynamics of consent. The legal and ethical implications of informed consent challenge practices of representation as they do sexual relations and medical interventions. Phyllis began an engagement with photography in the 1980s when ideas about the politics of representation informed critical documentary practices. When I ask her if she was interested in these debates, Phyllis tells me that she and her collaborators were drawn more to the traditional tenets of photojournalism — such as capturing the moment, or to photographic modernism's emphasis on the subjective rather than objective gaze and the sensuality of form. Yet the practices of photographers like Phyllis who were engaged in depicting their own communities

on the margins implicitly informed the intellectual reorientation of the photographic image in this period. Even when picturing your own, negotiating consent can be a complicated matter. As Phyllis's personal reflections suggest, many dykes wanted to be photographed and took great pleasure in describing and acting out their fantasies for camera. Likewise, the community wanted photographs, with readers of *On Our Backs* regularly writing in to ask for more images, or different images, to appear in the magazine. This reciprocal relationship between photographer, model, and reader, was not always straightforward but it was only through negotiation that lesbian photography developed. The work of Phyllis and her peers was also made in dialogue with a previous generation of lesbian photographers. As is often the case with intergenerational encounters, these relationships were largely supportive but not without their own antagonisms, as a new queer attitude sometimes jarred with lesbian feminist perspectives. A new lesbian aesthetic developed in the 1990s within a constellation of social ties and political affiliations, historical precedents and evolving discourses surrounding gender and sexuality.

Watching documentation of Phyllis at work shows the photographer and models engaging in a process of negotiation, which often needed to be spoken. While shooting three models in an alleyway for the film *Erotica: A Journey into Female Sexuality* (1997), one of them, lissaivy, had to pee. 'Now I was thinking that I'd love to photograph that,' Phyllis recalls, 'And all of a sudden, mid-stream, she asked me if I wanted to.' This spontaneous collaboration prompted the first photographs in *The Pee Series* (1997–2001). Its spirit is ongoing, and underwrites the images that appear in this book. When models signed releases for their images in the early 1990s, they could not have anticipated the vast differences of scale that separate the circulation and distribution of images online from their printed counterparts. Shifting experiences of identity, public life, or the right to private life, characterise the discussions that have taken place around each of the images that appear in the pages of *Dark Room*, under the sign of a political moment, a sexual identity, and have sometimes meant that reproduction is neither possible nor desirable.

The politicisation of queer sex during the onset of the HIV/AIDS crisis frames Phyllis's archive and the scenes that it documents. Alongside photographs that sought to expand visual languages for representing lesbian sexuality, Phyllis also documented the day-to-day activity of queer life in San Francisco. The culture wars of the US in the 1980s and 1990s, to which debates about pornography in feminist circles were closely and complexly related, created a context of oppressive censorship. The pernicious campaigns of Senator Jesse Helms, a Republican Congressional advocate on the Christian Right, were regularly covered in *On Our Backs*, from the high profile cancellation of Robert Mapplethorpe's retrospective 'The Perfect Moment' at the Corcoran Gallery of Art in Washington D.C. in 1989 to local events such as the confiscation of San Francisco photographer Jock Sturges's archive by the FBI in 1991. In the same issue in which *The Shoe Box* appears, a coupon suggests readers subscribe to the magazine in order to defeat Helms. A tick box allows readers to confirm that 'yes, I want to help defeat Jesse Helms' by including a $30 cheque for one year's subscription, $2 of which will be donated to the campaign of Harvey Gantt, who stood against incumbent Helms in the 1990 US Senate elections. Phyllis's photographs include various street protests and their overlapping political struggles, the violent lack of government response to the crises surrounding HIV/AIDS, state sanctioned homophobia and feminist campaigns for reproductive rights. These struggles are not confined to one particular group but reflect an entanglement of geographic specificities, economic realities, and urgent coalitions. In many of the photographs, women put their bodies on the line, confronting an increasingly militarised police force on the street and more insidious practices, like censorship, cancellation, and forced closure — for example of publications, exhibitions, and cruising sites, through which state power was maintained.

Importantly, the spaces of sex and protest that appear in Phyllis's photographs are also those in which photographs exchanged hands. Photography has an active life that far extends the uses it is put to in visual art. The images in this book circulated in magazines and as flyers, and were more likely to be found exhibited in a café than in a gallery. Many of the spaces recorded by Phyllis were lesbian-run, places to explore lesbian sexuality outside of the male gaze. In the context of the events described above, lesbian sex was recast as a public political act. This book reflects a period in which hard-won combination drug therapies and grassroots safe sex initiatives were transforming queer sexual practices and politics. During one ACT UP demonstration, Phyllis recalls a group of dykes showing up to the *On Our Backs* office and demanding that they participate in the production of a pornographic film. This resulted in the illegal commandeering of a university bathroom with a magazine staffer posted as lookout. *Bathroom Sluts* (1991) is directed by Lulu Belliveau, under the pseudonym Lulu Sanchez, with Phyllis on camera. Scenes are interleaved with stunning black and white photographs by Leon Mostovoy, whose important photo-essay *Market Street Cinema* (1987–88) shows the backstage comradeship between queer femmes who made their living as sex workers. *Bathroom Sluts* ends with a separate feature, a kind of 'how was it for you?' in which the participants reflect on the experience of making the film. One of them hopes that this document of queer lesbian sex will wind up in the Lesbian Herstory Archives in New York.

An intimate dialogue between desire and documentary sets the foundations of *Dark Room*. Print has been crucial for the circulation of lesbian images and for consolidating histories of lesbian photography at particular moments. In 2017, when Phyllis's work is shown as part of *On Our Backs: An archive*, an exhibition organised by artists Janina Sabaliauskaite and Jade Sweeting at The NewBridge Project, an artist run space in Newcastle, I write that, despite feeling a million miles away from the lesbian sex scene of San Francisco in the '90s, the inclement conditions of a post-industrial northern English city are no stranger place than anywhere else to come across these photographs. Print is a story of distributed media, reflecting many instances of what queer media historian Cait McKinney calls 'information activism' that connected disparate communities long before the internet did. What appears in this book has been made possible because of many moments of contact, shown in, and facilitated by, the photographs themselves. Each contact leaves a trace, in the images themselves, in the material conditions that facilitate our encounters with photographic archives, and in the many moving parts that make up the community through which queer photographic cultures continue to find meaning. Dealing with queer history often means dealing with nonsynchronous temporalities. As we're preparing material for this publication, I ask Phyllis if she can locate the issue of *DIVA* in which I first encountered her photographs. In the accompanying article, Phyllis talks to an interviewer about her desire for a book. 'The book is going to be just lesbian sex stuff that I've accumulated over the past ten years or so. It's really hard to market, because some of my work is considered really obscene, and I think some people are still afraid of it.' The preservation of queer culture is only possible through the making and remaking, collaboration and contestation, of queer community. It is to this ongoing work of labour and love that Phyllis Christopher's photographs bear a tender and fearless witness.

List of Works

Acknowledgements

With special thanks to all the models who appear in the pages of this book:

angus ann
Pamela August Russell
Dean Ayers
Cooper Lee Bombardier
Leigh Crow
Annika Dukes
Alison Gallant
Huckleberry
Jessica
Karin
Kris Kovick
Lex
lissaivy
Marcus
Molly McKay
Midori
Judith Moman
Michou Olivera
Lisa Palac
Shar Rednour
Laurie Sirois
Jack Strano
Stephanie
Terese Taylor
Tribe 8
Lex Vaughn
& those who remain anonymous

And to:

Kim Airs
Fiona Anderson
Irene Aristizábal
Mandy Baxter
Lulu Belliveau
Susie Bright
Helen Collard
Rosie Cooper
Rosen Eveleigh
Gavin Everall
Karen Everett
Laura Guy
Lizzie Homersham
Kas
Nan Kinney
Mason Leaver-Yap
Adam Lewis-Jacob
Kim McAleese
Alessandra Mondin
Strange Perfume
Jill Posener
Elsa Richardson
Janina Sabaliauskaite
Tamar Shlaim
Debra St. John
Debbie Sundahl
Kate Sweeney
Jade Sweeting
Michelle Tea
Michael White
Lillian Wilkie

Kickstarter Thanks

Adrian — Angèle & Fanny — Michele Allen — Tristessa Allison — Fiona Anderson — Linda Anderson — Gem Andrews — Gretchen L Anthony — Holly Argent — Mel Ashby — Chloe Atkins — edna azulay — Lynn Harris Ballen — Stacey Baumgarn — David Bayer — Taelor Beau — Annette Becker — Nuno Beijinho — Joey Bennett — Louise Benson — Jessy Berlanga — Lanee Bird — Sarah Rose Bird — Richard Bliss — E. E. Boucht — Dawn Bowman & Emma Hughes — Beth Bramich — Rosemary Bristow — Rachel Britton — James Brook — Alice Brooke — Gwyn Brookes — Clare Brown — Paige Brown — Sarah Brown — Renèe Helèna Browne — Katie Bruce — Eva Brunner — Burning House Books — Joanne Michelle Burke — Kat Bussey — Maria Elena Buszek — Stefano Campagna — Peter Campbell — M. Caron — Vincent Casalaina — Catrina and Huffty — Roisin Cavanagh — Sophie Chapman — Ryan Chernikoff — Neelybat Chestnut — french chris — Miarosa Ciallella — Chuck Clanton — Debra Cleaver — Kim Coleman — A. Collens — Phoebe Colley — Kate Conroy & Marty Correia — J. M. Cooper — Christie Costello — Meg Covington — Tristan Crane — Neil Crawford — Stefano Cremonesi — Ra Criscitiello — Martin Crowley — Eileen Cunningham — Curious Arts — Dan — Eoin Dara — Upasana Das — Nichola Davies — Deborah Deegan — Maria de Lima — Sid Deluca — Melanie DeMore — Tess Denman-Cleaver — Nyree Denney — Dante Desmond — Diana and Gaby — Jules Dill — Alice Dillon — Andy Dobler — Eamonn Dobson — Sam Dolbear — Dot and Krista — Saoirse Dryden — M DuBose — Jess T. Dugan — Jennifer Dumpert — Flora Dunster — The Dutchers — Tijanna O. Eaton — Ebianchi — Eddie — E&E — Jane Earnshaw — Kyra Edeker — JEB (Joan E. Biren) — Terri Elkin — C. Elliott — Boka En — Karen Everett — Katherine Fackrell — Adrianna Faliszewski — Batya Family — Emily Farrell — Anastasiia Fedorova — Ellen Ferwerda — Gina Fields — Hawt Flash — Genevieve Flavelle — David flynn — Amy Forrest — Natasha Fowler — Sparrow Fox — Sarah-Joy Ford — Steven Fraser — Maria Fusco — Gabrielle Garcia — Martha Garvey — Nora Gause — Diana Georgiou — Diane F. Germain — Ruth Gibbs — T. Gidseg — Gloria Glitzer — Sophie Goddard — i.f. Gonzales — Mimi Gonzalez — Sera Gonzalez — Theo Gordon — Phyllis Gorman — Patrick Graham — Catherine Grant — C.E. Gray — Marcus Green — Susie Green — Lewis greener — Kelso Gregory — Gabriella D. Guilfoil — Elís Gunnarsdóttir — Nicola Guy — Mace Guzman — H2 — R. J. Hall — Lucy Hammond — Suzanne Hardy — Em Hedditch — Dave Henderson — Nik Hendrikx — Liz Henry — lynne hepburn — Jill Heslop — Christa Hillhouse — Lubaina Himid — Louise Hipwell & Tanya Fyans — Fenella Hitchcock — Drew Hoffman — Jack Hogan — Sybil Holiday — Cara Holmes — Lizzie Homersham — Deanna A. Horvath — Lauren Houlton — Catherine Howe — Lesley Hoyt-Croft — Emma Hughes — Beverley Hunter — Bridget Iesan — Micah Ismach — Jac & Jes — Marcus Jack — Hubert Jaming — Trees Jansen — Jenny & Sarah — Joseph — JulieB — Sarah Jury — Ott Kagovere — Cynthia Kane — Sandi Kaplan — Brenda Keegan — Joshua M.arc Keller — Andi Kent — Ak knol — Sergey Kochergan — Izzy Kroese — Stefan Kruger — Taia Kwinter — Marcin Lakomski — Thomas Lambert — Lynn Lampky — Dovile Lapinskaite — Juana Lemus — Lenny — Sacha Lenz — zoe leonard — David Leszcynski — Gideon Leventhall — Airley — R. M. Lewis — Laurie Lezin-Schmidt — Andrea Lhotská — Linda — Katherine Lloyd — April Lombardo — Lisa Looye — Anna Lovelace — Annika's sexy older lover — Lyndsey Lupe — Anitra H. Lykke — Heidi Lypps — Katie Lynch — Alex M. — Simon Marsham — Cebastian Martinez — Mattia — Kim McAleese — Laura Mccall — Laura McCormick — Marcus E. McCrory — Sarah McEvans — Emily McGirr — Maura McGovern — Martin McGrath — Neil McGuire — Emma McIntyre — Molly McKay Williams — francis mckee — Ulla McKnight — Meera — Christian V. Mejia — Dawn Mellor — Midnight Memphis — Melanie A Mills — MiriamC — K. Bellamy Mitchell — Tuesday Mink Morningstar — Alessandra Mondin — Diane Montondo —

Alisa K. Moore — Matthew Moore — Cas Morris — Fiontán Moran — Jennifer Morris — K.G. Mumper — Paige Murphy — Kas N. — Heather Nelson — Sara Neville — JC Newman — Niamh — Amy Nicholson — Rosa Nussbaum — Wayne O. — Occasional Papers — Tanya Paperny — Jenni Olson — Jennifer Page — Kim Palagyi — Brooke Palmieri — Amy V. Paris — Mathew Wayne Parkin — K PATRICK & S MCINTYRE — Bridget Penney — Alex Peters — Dr Michael Petry — Claire Phillips — Angela Piccini — Belle Piec — Arto Polus — Cynthia Posey — Charlie Prodger — Jess Pumphrey — Jen Rainin & Franco Stevens — Emily Rawlins — Stephanie Reiley — Steve Reinke — Sonya Rhee — Rhiannon — Caitlin Rimmer — Carlos Rodriguez @ Queerspaces — Jane Rolo — Matthew Scott Roren — Michael A. Rosen — Roxy Rosen — Emily Rosenberg — Hannah Rosenfeld — Betty Lark Ross — Rebecca Rouse — Maxime Rowson & Caroline Roach — Victoria and David Ruderman — Hillary Russak — Pamela August Russell — Janina Sabaliauskaite — Safiah — Ava Sakal — Reem Saleh — Paul Sammut — Elizabeth Sargent — Joseph Morgan Schofield — Courtney Scott — Lori Selke — Andrea Sellers — Michele Serchuk — Asa Seresin — Erika Servin — Suzanne M. Shifflett — Elissa Silsbury — Nancy Silverrod — N Singh — Judy Ornelas Sisneros — Slick — Stef Smith — Laura Snoad — Giulia Spadafora — Lady Rachell Diane Spencer of Dunans Castle, Scotland — Juanita Spooner — P. Staff — Inta Stalidzane — Andrea Stanley — Suzannah Stason — Jelena Stojković — Zoe Strachan — Laura Stratton — Becky Swain — Jade Sweeting — Jessica Tanzer — Terese Taylor — Jude Thomas — Laura Thomas — Taralyn Thomas — Fid Thompson — lissaivy — Emery Kate Tillman — Fag Tips — Amy Tobin — Monique Todd — Rena Tom — A K Tosh — DJ Trainor — transgreaser — Egle Trezzi & Naïma Ben Ayed — Tom Truscott — Danny Valero — Lysa Irene Velásquez — Missy Vice — Helen Walkinshaw — Jay Carson Wallace — Bix Warden — Ed Webb-Ingall — Rachel Werther — Isaiah Whisner — Finley White — Viv White — Lillian Wilkie — Turner Willman — Carson Wolfe — Dawn Woolley — Ajamu X — Erin Yarborough — Sean Yendrys — linsey young — Zooik & those who wish to remain anonymous

Dark Room: San Francisco Sex and Protest, 1988–2003
by Phyllis Christopher

With contributions by Susie Bright, Phyllis Christopher, Laura Guy, Shar Rednour, and Michelle Tea

Edited by Laura Guy
Designed by Rosen Eveleigh
Photo edit by Phyllis Christopher and Laura Guy with Rosen Eveleigh
Commissioning Editor Lizzie Homersham
Published by Book Works
Distributed by Book Works, UK, and Idea Books, Netherlands
Typeset in Wei Huang's Arielvetica
Printed by robstolk in Amsterdam using Kamiko Suna 120gsm and Multicolor Mirabell 450gsm

ISBN: 978-1-912570-07-2

Book Works
19 Holywell Row
London EC2A 4JB
United Kingdom

Book Works receives National Portfolio funding from Arts Council England. Phyllis Christopher's work towards *Dark Room*, and an accompanying public programme, has been generously supported by an Arts Council England Developing Your Creative Practice grant. We also wish to thank BALTIC, Gateshead, and Grand Union, Birmingham, for additional support. This publication would not have been realised without the backers of our Kickstarter campaign, to whom we express deep gratitude.